THE PROBLEM WITH RULES

THE MALCOLM LESTER PHI BETA KAPPA LECTURES ON LIBERAL ARTS AND PUBLIC LIFE

DAVID A. DAVIS, EDITOR

THE PROBLEM WITH RULES

Essays on the Meaning and Value of Liberal Education

JOHN CHURCHILL

UNIVERSITY OF VIRGINIA PRESS
Charlottesville and London

University of Virginia Press

Printed in the United States of America on acid-free paper

First published 2021

9 8 7 6 5 4 3 2 1

Library of Congress Cataloging-in-Publication Data

Names: Churchill, John Hugh, author.
Title: The problem with rules : essays on the meaning and value of liberal education / John Churchill.
Description: Charlottesville : University of Virginia Press, 2021. | Series: The Malcolm Lester Phi Beta Kappa lectures on liberal arts and public life | Includes bibliographical references.
Identifiers: LCCN 2020037880 (print) | LCCN 2020037881 (ebook) | ISBN 9780813945774 (hardcover) | ISBN 9780813945781 (ebook)
Subjects: LCSH: Education, Humanistic. | Critical thinking. | Wittgenstein, Ludwig, 1889–1951. | Philosophy and education.
Classification: LCC LC1011 .C448 2021 (print) | LCC LC1011 (ebook) | DDC 370.11/2—dc23
LC record available at https://lccn.loc.gov/2020037880
LC ebook record available at https://lccn.loc.gov/2020037881

Cover design by Derek Thornton, Notch Design/background: Nadzeya Pakhomava/Shutterstock

CONTENTS

INTRODUCTION TO THE MALCOLM LESTER LECTURES

Mercer University hosts the Malcolm Lester Phi Beta Kappa Lectures on the Liberal Arts and Public Life each year as part of our Phi Beta Kappa induction ceremony. The lectures allow our students to meet an important figure in American higher education and to have conversations about the value of a liberal arts education. This experience reinforces the significance of the students' accomplishment in being inducted into Phi Beta Kappa, and the conversations can be inspiring, but a series of lectures and conversations among a small group of people only goes so far. Dr. Malcolm Lester had a vision for a series of lectures that supports the mission of the Phi Beta Kappa Society and that reaches a broad audience to influence the discourse about liberal arts in the United States.

Dr. Malcolm Lester, a 1945 graduate of Mercer, returned to Mercer after graduate school to teach history and was named dean of the College of Liberal Arts and Sciences in 1955. In 1959, he left Mercer to join the faculty of Davidson College, where he taught for the next thirty years. While at Davidson, he served as a Phi Beta Kappa senator and member of the Committee on Qualifications, which reviews schools' applications to shelter chapters of the Phi Beta Kappa Society. He felt strongly that Mercer should also shelter a chapter of Phi Beta Kappa, and he encouraged faculty to apply. In 2007, he made a gift for a lecture series on the liberal arts at Mercer to commence once Mercer sheltered a chapter of the Phi Beta Kappa Society, and Mercer received a charter in 2016. His bequest states that "the income of such endowed fund shall be used to pay for the delivery of and publication of an annual oration to be delivered by a distinguished scholar at the annual initiation of members in course of Phi Beta Kappa." The lectures will be published by the University of Virginia Press, as requested by Dr. Lester, who earned his PhD from the University of Virginia, where he was inducted into Phi Beta Kappa as a graduate student.

The lecture series focuses on the relationship between the liberal arts and public life, which has been contentious in the recent past. Many politicians have publicly disparaged liberal arts majors, including President Obama, who once dismissed the value of studying art history, and Senator Marco Rubio, who claimed that we need fewer philosophers. They often suggest that liberal arts degrees are of less economic value than vocational or professional programs. In the years following the Great Recession, most states significantly cut appropriations for higher education, and funding levels in many states are still below 2008 levels. Meanwhile, enrollment in many liberal arts programs has declined since 2008. A 2018 study from the American Enterprise Institute found that the number of undergraduates earning bachelor's degrees in some liberal arts subjects, such as English, history, and philosophy, fell by at least 15 percent between 2008 and 2016, even though the total number of bachelor's degrees rose 31 percent during that period. The data show that students are gravitating to applied sciences, engineering, and business, and many of them are following the conventional wisdom that these programs lead more predictably to careers with secure incomes. The fallout from this shift has had serious consequences for higher education. Enrollment in some liberal arts majors has declined, and some schools have eliminated liberal arts majors. Several schools have eliminated majors in philosophy and foreign languages, and others have cut or reduced core disciplines such as history and English or relegated humanities and social science programs to service components supporting more vocational programs. An even greater concern is the fact that dozens of small colleges specializing in liberal arts have closed or consolidated since 2008 due to low enrollment and declining revenue. Under the circumstances, it is unsurprising to see regular think pieces in major publications proclaiming the end of the liberal arts.

This situation requires us to think about the relationship between liberal arts and public life. We must ask if the liberal arts serve a useful or necessary purpose, if they are economically valuable, and if we should consider moving to different academic paradigms. Despite the current trends, numerous studies indicate that the liberal arts have considerable practical value. A 2014 study from the American Association of Colleges and Universities, for example, found that 93 percent of employers agree that a job candidate's demonstrated capacity to think critically, communicate clearly, and solve complex problems is more important than their undergraduate major. The contemporary workplace is a highly dynamic environment, and it requires and rewards skills that make people adaptable, creative, and collaborative, which are the skills that a liberal arts education develops. A study by the Mellon Foundation released in 2019, "The Economic Benefits and Costs of a Liberal Arts Education," finds that a liberal arts education leads to meaningful economic mobility, which has benefits both for the individuals in their earning ability and numerous positive benefits for society. Contrary to criticism, a liberal arts education makes a person employable and productive, and people with liberal arts degrees have a lifetime earning potential comparable with people in technical fields. The data, therefore, do not support the movement away from liberal arts in American universities. Instead, it reinforces the value of a liberal arts education for economic development at both the individual and the social level.

Economic impact, however, is a limited means to measure the value of an education, and it does not reflect many of the most important aspects of a liberal arts education, which are abstract yet highly valuable. Rather than a specific body of content knowledge, liberal arts and sciences education is a learning method that teaches students how to find, understand, interpret, and evaluate evidence and information according to scientific, social scientific, and humanistic perspectives. While a large range of academic disciplines are associated with the liberal arts, the crux of the method is interdisciplinary. It is a way of learning that privileges critical thinking, breadth of knowledge, exposure to divergent ideas and perspectives, ethical discernment, civic engagement, rational decision making, and lifelong learning. This valuable set of skills empowers a person to be an effective and adaptable worker and to live a free and content life in a civil society. A 2018 study by the

American Academy of Arts and Sciences, in fact, finds that people with liberal arts educations have high rates of satisfaction with their jobs and with their lives. A liberal arts education has value that benefits a person both quantitatively and qualitatively. Because some of the values are not obvious, however, we need to explain the learning methods to students choosing colleges and academic majors, we need to convince politicians and business leaders that a liberal arts education prepares people for productive careers, and we need to make the argument in public that the liberal arts are beneficial to individuals and society.

The Phi Beta Kappa Society is a leading voice advocating for the value and benefits of liberal arts and sciences education, fostering freedom of thought, and recognizing academic excellence. While one specific chapter of the society sponsors the Malcolm Lester Lectures, they reinforce the society's mission to advocate for the liberal arts. When the Lester Lectures committee convened to discuss the purpose of the lectures and to identify individuals who we felt could articulate the value and benefits of a liberal arts and sciences education, we immediately agreed on one person to inaugurate the lectures and set the tone for the series, Dr. John Churchill. As executive secretary of the Phi Beta Kappa Society for fifteen years, he led the society's efforts to support liberal education and raise public awareness about the value of the liberal arts through the arts and sciences initiative. Dr. Churchill's life was a testament to the importance of the liberal arts. He was born in Hector, Arkansas, and grew up in Little Rock. He attended Southwestern at Memphis, now Rhodes College, where he was inducted into Phi Beta Kappa, and he then studied at the University of Oxford as a Rhodes Scholar and Yale University, where he earned his PhD in 1977. He taught philosophy at Hendrix College in Conway, Arkansas, and was vice president for Academic Affairs and dean of the college for seventeen years before being named executive secretary of the Phi Beta Kappa Society in 2001. He passed away in 2019, and his wife, Jean, and three adult children and nine grandchildren survive him.

Dr. Churchill's lectures, *The Problem with Rules,* reveal an apparent paradox in any attempt to explain rational methods, such as rules, regulations, instructions, or recipes. This paradox forces us to acknowledge the reliance of such methods on an implicit set of customs and practices that are rooted in patterns of human uptake and response—capacities of "seeing as" and "taking for" without which our capacities of language and reasoning would not exist. His lectures interrogate the fundamental methods of liberal education. The liberal arts, he argues, lack foundations. They are a method for deliberation, but the rules of deliberation are not stable. Instead, they are based on arbitrary criteria, such as relevance or preference, but as we select these arbitrary criteria, we examine ourselves. He advocates for openness in our deliberation to encourage us to consider diverse perspectives as we formulate arguments based on our own preferences. One of the most important messages of Dr. Churchill's lectures is that the interdisciplinary liberal arts method of finding, understanding, and evaluating evidence can be used to examine the liberal arts itself. As a philosopher, Dr. Churchill believed that self-examination was important so that we could understand the fundamental principles of our knowledge and our judgement.

The Malcolm Lester Lectures will provide an important platform for thought leaders in the liberal arts to articulate the role of the liberal arts in public life. While many people would see this value as self-evident, the social and political opposition to liberal arts education indicates that we need to explain how liberal arts and sciences education works, why it matters, and how people benefit from it. The Lester Lectures committee anticipates that this series will offer important contributions to the ongoing discourse about the liberal arts and public life, and we are grateful for our partnership with the University of Virginia Press to make this possible.

DAVID A. DAVIS

FOREWORD

John Churchill's untimely death in November of 2019 left this book complete but unfinished, like a freshly turned baseball bat lacking stain and varnish. We—John's son and brother—undertook the task of replying to readers' comments and making revisions we thought John himself would have undertaken had he lived to do so. Our revisions were minor and consisted primarily of providing signals to aid readers' navigation between chapters. The heart of each chapter is John's work alone, but we are responsible for any residual flaws in the varnish.

We have both heard John talk on many occasions about the ideas presented here. They were central to his professional and personal life, and we are honored to be a very small part of helping them find published form. His life, like this book, was marked by eclectic genius, an abundance of goodwill and a deeply humane spirit. We thank David Davis at Mercer University and Eric Brandt at the University of Virginia Press for their generosity, support, and encouragement on this journey to publication. We thank our extended family for their love, confidence in us, and steadfast encouragement.

This is a book in which style of presentation mirrors the subject. Deliberation is described as a signature skill nourished by liberal education; the tone and style of the book invite deliberation, and the rhetorical strategies John uses exhibit it. It is not just *about* liberal education; it is an *embodiment* of such an education. Nowhere is this clearer than in the tactics used to analyze the subject under consideration. As John writes, "We proceed in one among many directions, constantly gesturing back, forward, and to the side toward tangent topics, anticipating, reminding, warning the reader that this or that topic will look different or make sense when we see it again with more and different mileage behind us." This nonlinear approach is necessary because sentence and paragraph structures are catenarian, with the chain-like features of words and phrases suggesting a sequential logic as the best method to unpack the topic. John's image is rather one of moving around the periphery of a circle and reentering the territory at different angles, as one might enter a city on different pathways to explore it. It is the assemblage of all this crisscross mapping that will give us the best view. The reader would do well to remember that the guidance John gives across this terrain is meant not only to correctly designate the sites but to puzzle, to entice and entertain. The journey is as often enticing and humorous as it is instructive. This, too, is part of what it means to explore the meaning and value of the liberal arts, which engage a large range of our human sensibilities.

We write amid a pandemic that is surely accelerating the profound transformation of American higher education that

John emphasizes in his preface. Shouldn't discussions of the value of a liberal arts education wait until the emergency has passed? No, the current context has given such discussions even more urgency. As the world fights a new disease and millions become unemployed and go hungry because of the fight, John's preface provides an example of the enduring practicality of the liberal arts. Writing in the year before the pandemic, he asks, "Do the liberal arts help feed the world? Probably not. Do they cure diseases? Likely not. But if questions need to be asked about the relative merits of feeding the world, curing diseases . . . the liberal arts will help." The current tension between reopening the economy and suppressing the spread of infection—that is, between the relative merits of feeding the world and curing diseases—has the best hope of humane resolution through liberal arts–enabled deliberation.

HUGH O. H. CHURCHILL

LARRY R. CHURCHILL

PREFACE

We are a couple of decades deep into one of the great transformative periods in American higher education, a period comparable to the sweep of small liberal arts colleges across the Midwest and South in the late nineteenth century, the early twentieth century emergence of the research university model, and the headlong growth after World War II, as the GI Bill and subsequent baby boomers fueled vast expansion. But things are different now. Baby boomers, long out of college, are retiring. Their generational echo has passed through college. The current transitions are not like any we have seen before.

Every aspect of higher education is undergoing profound change. There are more students, of more richly varied ethnicity, more widely distributed in age and degree of preparation, with a growing female majority, and with increasingly vocational aims. There are more institutions, of more varied types, and they are often more complex, with multiple foci. Sources of funding are shifting. There is more borrowing and hence more debt, more discounting, less state support, and in most cases, rising tuition. There are for-profits and online institutions. The faculties' connection to the college or university is being realigned. Numbers vary according to the reporter, but there can be no doubt that the traditional paradigm of instruction conducted by full-time tenured or tenure-track faculty is no longer the experience of the typical American undergraduate. The contents of curricula are changing. The apparent choices and preferences of students are shifting. Political pressures are heavier and more sharply defined. The financing of higher education, viewed from the perspective of a legislature, a board of trustees, or a family, is in crisis. The word that turns up again and again as a descriptor of all this is "unsustainable."

So there is a set of changes that are, in the very nature of things, unpredictable, whose outcome is unknowable. Remember that in the year 1350 people didn't sit around saying hopefully, "Gee, the Middle Ages are a drag, but, you know, the Renaissance is just around the corner!" Kierkegaard wrote, "It is perfectly true, as the philosophers say, that life must be understood backwards. But they forget the other proposition, that it must be lived forwards."[1] If there is to be a "new normal," it is not clear what it will be. But it may involve a radically diminished middle class, a damaged middle class, a middle class without the confidence in progress and improvement that has characterized the American attitude toward education and incapable of supporting the institutions now thought of as indispensable. The impacts on institutions large and small, public and private, are very real, and they are not good.

No one has a precise or comprehensive grasp of what these changes are doing to American higher education. But it is safe to say that the liberal arts are in special jeopardy. They are in jeopardy because in an age of insistence on practical results they have been misunderstood as useless ornamentation. If the liberal arts are more than decorative frills, that needs to be stated. If they have an indispensable role, that needs to be insisted upon. If the institutions that nurture the liberal arts need to be supported in that cultivation, that too needs to be recognized and acted upon.

It is important to see that vagueness and contention go all the way down in the liberal arts. When the reality is vague, an insistence on precision can only lead to falsification. The liberal arts are the disciplines whose pursuit consists in the detection and appreciation of meaning in human affairs, in reflection on meaning's emergence. What would count as success in such pursuit? Understanding meanings, "getting" significances, appreciating values are accomplishments of very different sorts than mastering principles of accounting. We should not expect them to be demonstrable or measurable in the same ways. Some advocates of the liberal arts grasp the nettle and declare that they are not measurable at all, that when we try to measure them, we squeeze out the life and measure—at best—a side effect or a dried-out husk, not what we wanted to detect. Yet that plea seems counterproductive, as it is the prologue to a second claim: that the liberal arts are repositories of intrinsic value, necessarily disconnected from the grubby getting and spending of the material world, and must be valued in their own right and on their own terms or not at all. This is a splendid stance, but it is wrong and ultimately self-defeating in a context in which the liberal arts' glorious self-immolation might be widely greeted with enthusiastic approbation. In fact, the liberal arts are intimately related to the practical world, but the connection is subtler than we might think.

ENDS, MEANS, AND REFLECTION ON THE EMERGENCE OF MEANING

To adopt an end is to assign value to its achievement. To identify any process as the means to be undertaken in pursuit of that end is to assign that process a value derived from the end to which it will lead. The liberal arts are systematic, disciplined reflection on the assignment of values—the adoption of ends and of means to pursue them. The liberal arts are about deciding what to want and how to secure it. This is why the liberal arts can be unsettling; they hold the potential to challenge every stipulation about ends and means.

What useful work is there to be done in the consideration of ends and means? How do ends emerge? Are they "natural" or "given"? Is there some one big, final end that gives meaning to the rest? How would we know? Are all the partial ends that people pursue—say, wealth, fame, health, peace of mind, and pleasure—mutually compatible, or do alternative ends compete with each other, necessitating choice? If choice is necessary, can it be made rationally? Can it be done better or worse? How could we tell if someone got such a choice wrong? Are there ends that people choose that are simply wrong in themselves? Do people ever choose wrong ends, or do they only seem to choose evil, mistaking it for good? If people really want the ends they choose to pursue, why do they do things that frustrate those purposes? We would be justified in ignoring these questions only if we knew that we had the answers to them.

A parallel set of questions pertains to the choice of means, with an added set besides. Those pertain to efficiency, side effects, and unintended consequences. The phenomenon of global climate change illustrates the gravity of these considerations beyond any need for further explication. But we can bring them up at all only if we are capable of stepping outside the framework defined by the ends and means in question and exploring consequences that were, from the inside, either invisible or irrelevant. It is this suspension of the presumed rules of relevance that makes the liberal arts so chaotic, because they raise issues outside the focus of our pursuit.

After all the technical issues are settled, questions about value and meaning remain. For that reason, society has a stake in maintaining a reservoir of expertise in raising, articulating, and pursuing such "irrelevancies." Do the liberal arts help feed the world? Probably not. Do they cure diseases? Likely not. But if questions need to be asked about the relative merits of feeding the world, curing diseases, curbing population growth, keeping the peace, and myriad other worthwhile ends, the liberal arts will help. They are the windows on meaning.

"It is difficult to get the news from poems, yet men die miserably every day for lack of what is found there," writes William Carlos Williams in "Asphodel." Surely what Williams means is not that the lack of what is found in poems causes men and women to die but that it causes their deaths to be miserable ones. That is, people die without having "gotten it," without having caught on to a sense of things, for lack of what is found in poems. Deaths that could have come in the fullness of realization of the sense of things—or of some sense of things—come instead in emptiness, in a lack of meaning. Perhaps what justifies the liberal arts after all is the hope that, through these reflections on meaning and value, though we must die, there is a better chance that we will not die miserably.

A NOTE ON THE TEXT

This book derives principally from the inaugural Malcolm Lester Lectures, delivered at Mercer University on April 5–6, 2018. An earlier version of a portion of chapter 2 was presented to the annual meeting on the American Conference of Academic Deans on January 24, 2013, in Atlanta, Georgia. The material in chapter 5 was presented in the inauguration festivities of William Craft as the president of Concordia College in Moorhead, Minnesota, on April 29, 2012, and appeared in the college's alumni/ae magazine. A version of the concluding chapter, chapter 6, was published in *College Literature*, February 1991.

THE PROBLEM WITH RULES

1

THE "ESSENCE" OF LIBERAL EDUCATION

THIS BOOK DEVELOPS AN understanding of the meaning and value of the liberal arts inspired by the work of Ludwig Wittgenstein. This inspiration extends to both the major ideas of the book and the methodology for presenting these ideas. In this chapter and the one that follows I will describe the reversal in Wittgenstein's approach to philosophy that is most instructive for how we understand the arts and sciences. It would be a mistake to read these chapters as some sort of scholarly exegesis that is then applied to liberal education. Rather, my aim is to show that a compelling and transformational view of liberal education can be developed by following some of Wittgenstein's insights and methods. I will be using the terms "the liberal arts," "arts and sciences," and "liberal education" interchangeably. Sometimes people try to distinguish among them, but those distinctions seem to me artificial and forced and for my purposes here unimportant.

Contemporary readers of Ludwig Wittgenstein's *Philosophical Investigations* must be struck by the way in which the philosopher's explanation of his book cries out for hypertext a half century before its invention. It is an album of sketches, he writes, that resists a single linear arrangement. There are jumps from one topic to another; the exigencies of the arrangement require that closely related topics be widely separated; the exposition repeatedly crisscrosses over a terrain, constantly recognizing new connections and new aspects of familiar objects. Understanding, as he says elsewhere, "dawns slowly over the whole" rather than proceeding as the full illumination of one object followed by the full illumination of what is logically next. Many paths have a claim to be "the way through," and since showing that is a part of the point of the work, it would be a falsification to pretend otherwise in the exposition. A certain framework of expectations can make this sort of procedure intensely frustrating. But it pays off.

Reliant as this book is on Wittgenstein's work, I have followed something of the same principle, though in muted fashion. This book does follow a linear progression. I begin with a consideration of Wittgenstein's life and work through the lenses of liberal education. I then examine the well-known ends of liberal education through the lenses of Wittgenstein's work. Then I take up perennial topics of curriculum and pedagogy. The big conclusion is to affirm that a perspective shaped by Wittgenstein's insights can show us why and how we need humanistic knowledge and values—a vision of humanity's place in the world.

But this linearity of plotline is misleading. Practically everything is presupposed at every turn. There is no pretense of an

Archimedean point of leverage, a Cartesian indubitable, or a Platonic Form to ground our inquiry. We begin, as we always must, in medias res. We proceed in one among many directions, constantly gesturing back, forward, and to the side toward tangent topics, anticipating, reminding, warning the reader that this or that topic will look different or make sense when we see it again with more and different mileage behind us. These tactics are concessions to the necessity of showing in language that is necessarily linear, as words concatenate into sentences and sentences line up sequentially as paragraphs and so on, the character of a thought or set of thoughts that is not itself essentially linear at all but is susceptible of being imaged in any number of incompatible and perhaps complementary ways. That this is also the character of human knowledge is part of the big point of this work.

A TALE OF TWO PREFACES

Through his entire career, Wittgenstein focused on a single question, but he gave two very different answers. In fact, he gave two different kinds of answer. The greatest accomplishment of his work lies in the discovery and development of the second answer. It was a kind of answer so different from the kind of philosophical answers philosophers have typically sought that it remains, really, to be seen whether his work can be usefully appropriated within the tradition he sought to change, or whether philosophers will go on ignoring or misconstruing his work in the very mistaken modes he tried to correct. It is the kind of answer he gave, in his so-called "later" work, that makes him such an interesting philosophical figure in the task of understanding liberal education. The best way to compare the kinds of answer he gave, early and late, is to look at the prefaces of the two books *Tractatus Logico-Philosophicus* and *Philosophical Investigations.*

The *Tractatus Logico-Philosophicus* is a classic of philosophical writing. It is a work of such clarity and consistent inconsistency that it shows, on close study, the impossibility of its own conclusions and the impossibility of a whole way of doing philosophy. After the *Tractatus,* it is possible to look back and see what is fundamentally wrong with the traditions that go back to Descartes, to Spinoza, to Kant and Hegel, and to see the other problems in the tradition that runs from Locke through Hume to Wittgenstein's contemporary Bertrand Russell. The *Tractatus* derives this power from the elegance and simplicity of Wittgenstein's thought, its reduction of issues to a clear, well-defined essence. Wittgenstein knew that his work was clear and bold. The preface might well be a study in arrogance: he tells the reader that the book deals with "problems of philosophy," presumably all of them—in a book of ninety pages, lightly sprinkled with typescript. He says that he resolves these problems finally and absolutely. He says he shows that the reason these problems have been posed at all is confusion on the part of those who have wrestled with them and that the method of disposing of them is to expose them as nonsensical. With the demonstration that the concerns of generations of the world's best minds have been sheer nonsense, Wittgenstein presumably closes the issues forever by telling us that what we cannot talk about with sense, we must simply keep quiet about. And a shroud of pure silence falls over the whole enterprise. For the book's content is, by its own affirmation, just nonsense.

In what follows we will see some of the detail of the argument to end all argument. But for now it is enough to see that Wittgenstein wants an answer with these properties:

1. It must be comprehensive, applying to everything without exception.
2. It must be final, leaving no room for follow-up, clarification, or elaboration.
3. It must be unassailable, definitively and indisputably correct.

One of the marks of the overwhelming genius with which Wittgenstein pursued an answer of this kind is that he made it disappear upon completion. If you wanted to raise quibbles, you were out of bounds: clarity lay in silence, and to raise questions was only to demonstrate one's incomprehension. The great Indian philosopher Nagarjuna tried something similar in famously asserting the emptiness of all views about reality.[1] Wittgenstein goes this one better by claiming the field of victory as he leaves it.

By contrast, the preface to *Philosophical Investigations* is a congeries of qualifications and disclaimers. He says he'd rather not have published the book at all—and he did die before its publication, so that this and virtually all his other post-*Tractatus* writings came out posthumously. He says it's not, properly speaking, a book at all, but a kind of album, or collection of sketches. It lacks a single argumentative skein that is stated, developed, and at last restated in fullness of meaning. It doesn't cycle back to a beginning like the self-feeding river of *Finnegan's Wake*. Its action is more like the dissipation of a mountain river in the desert—with the added feature that its waters bubble back up uncontrollably everywhere.

As an exemplar of the kind of answers that philosophers ought to hope for, *Philosophical Investigations* implies—though it characteristically nowhere states at this level of generality:

1. There are no comprehensive and all-encompassing answers to anything, because the perspective from which such

answers would develop is an illusion, and we need to get over the idea of seeking it and the kind of answers it would provide.

2. All the answers that can be provided for any philosophical question are conditioned by the occasion in which they are posed and by the culture and intellectual preoccupations of those who undertake to produce the answers. So there cannot be answers that leave no room for follow-up, clarification, or elaboration.

3. The ground upon which available answers to philosophical questions rest is a matrix of agreement in action and in judgment that—on any particular occasion—will reflect some combination of innate human elements, cultural conditioning, and individual choice. Which of these, and to what degree, and what variant forms of them underlie cases of human agreement? It is impossible to provide a general answer, though sorting through particular cases should now be the central way of philosophizing.

And so the sort of inquiry philosophy is, and the effect it can have on ancillary questions like "What is the nature and end of liberal arts education?" cannot be what the author of the *Tractatus* thought. Philosophical work can, at best, help to remove confusions that are local and particular. It can help us work through occasional and specific obstacles. This contribution may be of extraordinary importance. But philosophy cannot provide answers that are comprehensive, final, or unassailable.

Analogously, philosophical reflection on liberal education should not hope to explain an educational format that promises students some sort of unconditional comprehensiveness, finality, or unassailability. Rather, in recognition of the conditional and provisional nature of all knowing, that reflection should help us understand education that strives toward more comprehension without the illusion that things can be completed, that seeks better answers without the illusion of the attainability of a last word, and that prepares for continuing argument and deliberation, not a thundering conclusion. It is that conception of the liberal arts that I will explore.

I do not intend, in this writing, to give an account of Wittgenstein's influence on those who teach and write philosophy. Instead, my aim is to explore a topic that has been, I believe, almost entirely unexamined: What is the relevance of the philosophical work of Ludwig Wittgenstein to the project of understanding the nature and aims of liberal education?

WILLIAM JAMES AND *THE VARIETIES OF RELIGIOUS EXPERIENCE*

Late in the nineteenth century, a Scottish jurist, Adam Lord Gifford, made a bequest to the four ancient universities of Scotland—Edinburgh, Glasgow, St. Andrews, and Aberdeen—for a series of lectures in "natural theology," the study of God as evidenced in the natural world, apart from any special revelation. First delivered in 1888, the Gifford Lectures are a late expression of the Scottish Enlightenment, and despite the somewhat dated conception, remain one of the most prestigious forums for wide-ranging philosophical exploration. Alfred North Whitehead delivered his *Process and Reality* as Gifford Lectures at Edinburgh in 1927–28. Other lecturers have included theologians such as Reinhold Niebuhr and Karl Barth; historians Arnold Toynbee and Herbert Butterfield; philosophers A. J. Ayer, Ian Barbour, and Simon Blackburn; writers such as Iris Murdoch; and scientists such as Sir Arthur Eddington and Werner Heisenberg. John Dewey, Sir J. G.

Frazer, Paul Tillich, and Martha Nussbaum have also been Gifford lecturers. Being a Gifford lecturer has been described by Jacques Barzun as "the highest honor in a philosopher's career."[2]

In 1901–2, Williams James delivered *The Varieties of Religious Experience* as Gifford Lectures, in Edinburgh. Widely regarded as the most distinguished and accessible of the entire series, James's lectures were published in 1902 and became virtually an instant classic. Among their readers was the young, struggling Austrian prodigy Ludwig Wittgenstein.

Though regarded as one of the preeminences of American pragmatism (along with Charles Sanders Pierce and John Dewey), James made his mark in medicine and then in the attempt to link physiology and psychology. His *Principles of Psychology* in two volumes, which also attracted Wittgenstein's attention, also became a classic. But it is *The Varieties of Religious Experience,* linking so much of James's own struggles with depression to his analytic and descriptive abilities, that remains his major contribution. In it, he not only offers a wide-ranging survey of religious attitudes and emotions, but he also defines the field of study in a novel way—a way that had profound influence on Wittgenstein, and a way that that can be of great value in our examination of liberal education.

Since the time of Plato, the question of what anything is has been understood as a search for its essence. It is this essentialism that drives early dialogues like the Euthyphro and the Phaedo. It reaches its most explicit expression in the Symposium, where the gaze of the philosopher is directed from beautiful objects on earth through various forms of unseen beauty until it reaches the essential Beauty itself, participation in which makes all the lesser forms of beauty themselves beautiful, to a degree. Implicit in this argument is, of course, the doctrine of the Forms, those essences which taken together supply a nature to all things. Socrates is so successful as Plato's representative in pressing this view that despite problems presented in Plato's own *Theaetetus* (and repeated in Aristotle's *Metaphysics*), it and its descendants have dominated the question ever since. Indeed the force of idealism, as this doctrine is known, is such that those who reject it have usually been obliged to fight off charges of nihilism or irrationality.

But James rejects it out of hand as he enters his examination of religion. He writes, "The word 'religion' cannot stand for any single principle or essence but is rather a collective name."[3] Seeking to guard against "the theorizing mind" and its tendency "always to the oversimplification of its materials," James urges that we "admit freely . . . that we may very likely find no one essence but many characters which may alternately be equally important to religion" (*VRE* 27). It follows that there would be no one specific and essential kind of religious object, emotion, or act (*VRE* 29).

In this approach James approximates Wittgenstein's concept of "family resemblance." By means of that concept, Wittgenstein accounts for the meaning of general terms without invoking essences but by appealing to the presence of many overlapping features, different mixtures being adequate for the applicability of the concept, and none being essential.[4] On M Street in Georgetown, Washington, DC, there is a barbecue restaurant that places a collection of six bottles of barbecue sauce on each table. They are labeled "Memphis," "Kansas City," "West Texas," and so on. They vary in degrees of hotness, sweetness, and sourness. Some are tomato based; others incorporate vinegar. They contain different kinds of chilis. It is entirely possible that there is no common ingredient shared by them all. But are they all barbecue sauces? Certainly. Is anyone inclined to charge that this place doesn't know what a barbecue sauce is? Surely not.

These sauces exemplify what Wittgenstein called "family resemblance." Frustrated in our attempt to designate an essence of liberal education, we may begin to fear we don't know what the term means. But if instances of liberal education are related by family resemblance rather than by shared possession of a common essence, our disagreements may look less dire, or even hopeful. Wittgenstein's contention was that the common concepts of everyday life are like this—language, game, play—as are the grand concepts of deep reflection: justice, good, truth. So the concept of liberal education is in good company.

What evidence is there that Wittgenstein was intimately acquainted with James's *Varieties of Religious Experience,* indeed, that he read and reread it? He cites it as an important influence on his thought in a letter to Bertrand Russell, on June 22, 1912.[5] His enlistment in the Austro-Hungarian army was at least partly motivated by a desire to experience the transformative power of confronting death, a theme that looms large in James. And decades later, he recommends the book to M. C. Drury as an essential book.[6] So it seems plausible to suppose that James is the source of this insight.

It seems likely that "family resemblance," often regarded as a trademark feature of his later thought, in fact has its origin in these passages from James. Whether or not this attribution of origin is in fact sound, the de facto correspondence of James's treatment of religion with Wittgenstein is indisputable. As is the de facto correspondence of the concept "liberal arts" with the doctrine of family resemblance.

A quick review—preparatory to exploration in the following chapter—of the varieties of "liberal arts" will bear this out.

VERSIONS OF THE LIBERAL ARTS

Perhaps the oldest version of "liberal arts" is the notion of "artes liberales," the skills demarcating, or appropriate to, a free person. But there is already ambiguity. Are the artes liberales those skills that a person, being free, will find useful in the pursuit of the activities that free people (as opposed to slaves and prisoners) undertake? Or are they the skills the acquisition of which make one free? The former is a notion about equipping oneself for a position in the world; the latter is an acquisitional idea embodying some vision of human well-being, what it consists in, and how to acquire it.

Cutting across the grain of this distinction is another, bearing on the efficacy of the material actually dealt with in liberal education. Is the point the accumulation of a certain quantity of general knowledge—a sort of literary or library-like effect, such that devotion to the right texts, say, the literary humanism curriculum at Oxford, or "classics" more broadly, brings it about that one becomes liberally educated? This seems to be the assumption behind the occasional expressions of outrage that a BA degree can be achieved at this college or that without a scrap of exposure to, say, Shakespeare or Chaucer or economic theory or what have you. Such outcries make you wonder about the magical efficiency of such exposure, but those excited by curriculum per se are seldom drawn to subtler cases of failure.

Or is the point that it is not general knowledge so much as generalizable skills that are the aim of liberal education?

Lists of such skills are readily available in college catalogs or easily derivable from their texts. A typical one would include the ability to deal with varieties of irresolution, such as doubt, uncertainty, vagueness, ambiguity, contingency, diversity, and paradox. And, it should be added, not to be paralyzed by them. Placing such skills as the primary aim makes the choice of materials a secondary, instrumentalist choice. The curriculum should consist of whatever materials are best suited to produce such outcomes. Thus the Yale Reports of 1828 concluded that the traditional, rote instruction-based curriculum of studying the classical languages and literatures was the most appropriate course of study for liberal learning because it conduced most readily to the acquisition of skills of intellectual agility. (More on this in the next chapter.) In this way a progressive conception of aims can lead to a traditionalist, or even regressive, stance as to means and methods.

Yet another admixture of proximal and distal aims is found in the claims of the pre-Socratic Sophists—in some ways the earliest advocates of the "liberal arts without essences." There are several well-known Sophists, but the most prominent is Protagoras, who taught that "Humanity (anthropos) is the measure of all things," or in other words, truth is what people are likeliest to agree on, and the method of seeking truth is, roughly, dialectic, a process of inquiry using language and argument. Like the other Sophists, Protagoras claimed to be able to train young men to be effective orators, that is, to defend themselves in the public courts. In a word, Protagoras claimed to be capable of teaching citizenship—how to be an independent and successful advocate of one's own views in public. While this seems a noble motive, it does not take much imagination to see it morphing into a defense of relativism, the view that there is no truth and that what he offers to teach is how make any position appear the best one. The Sophists were in fact accused of just this—by Plato—and that was a two-thousand-year near deathblow to their reputation. But their position does show the connection between liberal arts, intellectual skills, and citizenship.

Marcus Aurelius also shared this link, as Martha Nussbaum has done so much to show in her writing, though she, as he did, elevated citizenship to a cosmopolitan level, arguing that human and humane universals draw all people everywhere together in one community of dialogues, approached, of course, through liberal arts.

What this informal survey shows is that there is a concept of liberal arts that comprises many variants, resembling each other more or less in their possession of a set of characteristics shared to some degree with other versions. Though no characteristic may be shared by all versions, and perhaps no version possesses them all, still, different versions of liberal education cohere through the overlapping and repetition of the elements. Of course, there will be borderline cases. There will be educational enterprises and visions of the educated person about which we may rightly be uncertain whether they constitute liberal education. But that does not mean we do not know what liberal education is; it is because we recognize that case for what it is: a borderline case. That means the concept is to some degree vague, lacking precise boundaries. But so are the vast majority of concepts of everyday life. As we will see in a following chapter, Wittgenstein's view is that "exact" is simply praise and "inexact" criticism. The question is whether the concept is so inexact as to be useless. Anyone who demands concepts sharply enough bounded to resolve all borderline cases has not reflected sufficiently on the inexpungable vagueness of life.

So we can begin with an—at least potentially—happy pluralism. This is a characteristically American predicament, in that we are given vague and multifarious goods that everyone can specify to his own liking. You may not like my specifications and I may not like yours. But each of us is free to advocate his own and to associate with allies. Each of us may contend that the other's version is incomplete or just wrong. Or even perverse. One of us may be right. We will change our minds as we argue and deliberate. But if we are friends in Aristotle's sense—interested in advancing each other's conceptions of the good for his own sake—we will do so in good spirit and with some sense of common purpose.

Embracing pluralism does not imply indifference to further specifications. For example, I would argue that it matters a great deal that certain disciplines, their content, their methods, their histories, and their relations with other disciplines, are included in our conception of liberal education. Among them are philosophy, history, literature, religious studies, the social sciences and foreign languages, physics, and mathematics. If others disagree, I respect their positions in the context of pluralism, but I believe they are wrong, and must argue against them. My arguments will rely on a conception of human fulfillment. Similarly, it matters not just that liberally educated people can do something or other; there are specific things they are able to do, like deliberate. I will justify this assertion in chapters ahead.

At last, our question "What is liberal education?" is itself a liberal arts sort of question. It is a discussion question, not multiple choice or fill in the blank. It is an occasion for the exercises of the very skills and capacities we are describing as constituting the liberally educated person. Our arguments will be good ones if we bring to them lots of knowledge, lots of care about things that matter, and lots of skill in deliberation and communication. Our arguments will be happy ones if we revel in multiple perspectives and can be comfortable with ambiguity, uncertainty, and disagreement. The question "What is liberal education?" is not only about its subject matter. It is an instance of it.

THE DANGERS OF RATIONALIZING LIBERAL EDUCATION

Let me offer four versions of a comment on the adaptation of means and ends, all cast in terms of a travel metaphor. From the great English philosopher of the seventeenth century Francis Bacon we have this thought, drawn from his *Novum Organum:* "When a man runs the wrong way, the more active and swift he is, the further he will go astray."[7] The second version is the "father of modern philosophy," René Descartes, Bacon's near contemporary: "The greatest minds are capable of the greatest vices as well as the greatest virtues, and those who proceed very slowly may, provided they follow the straight road, really advance much faster than those who, though they run, forsake it."[8] Third, on the authority of Martin Gardner, dean of Lewis Carroll scholars, I offer this piece of rabbinical wisdom, oddly sometimes misattributed to Lewis Carroll (the upshot of an exchange between Alice and the grin of the Cheshire Cat amounts to the same thought): "If you don't know where you're going, any road will do."[9] Finally, there is the statement attributed to Yogi Berra, the great New York Yankees catcher and manager: "If you don't know where you're going, you're likely to end up someplace else." The double indeterminacy of Berra's version, in which an unspecified end is contrasted with a second, equally unspecified end, surpasses the others and ends up merging profundity with incoherence. My point is this: there are issues about what we know we want and how we propose to get them that transcend issues about efficiency and effectiveness. I propose to show that those issues are inexpungable from intentional activity and that we neglect them at our peril.

If there is a single characteristic that differentiates so-called modern societies from traditional or premodern ones, it is the readiness of modernity to countenance or even to demand the restructuring of social and economic relations according to the dictates of rationally conceived means/ends relationships. Science, or capitalism or engineering, identifies an end—be it truth, profit, or technique—and methodically, rationally, directs effort with increasing efficiency to achieve it. This intentional adaptation of means to accomplish designated ends, as a cultural imperative, is responsible for much of what we regard as "progress" in human affairs. It built the transcontinental railroads and put humans on the moon. It created the internet and the world financial structure. It drives advances in every department of human endeavor. Our world could not be conceived without it. A fair proportion of what is called "conservative" thought consists in praising its effects in the world, while a fair proportion of what is called "liberal" thought consists in worrying about them.

Here are a piece of praise and a piece of worry. First, modern rationalization of means/ends relationships in pursuit of the more efficient accomplishment of human goals is simply a refined version of the exercise of practical reason. It is the characteristic human facility. It is simply in us to do this, and we are most human when we are doing it. So there can be no question of regretting means/ends rationalization as a comprehensively bad thing. It's here to stay.

However, unless we have at any given moment infallibly conceived our ends and perfectly implemented our means, we are apt to be wreaking untold, unintended damage somewhere, somehow. The better we get at refining our means to reach our ends, and the greater the compass of such rationalized activities becomes in our lives, the graver the consequences of such shortcomings will become. Identifying an end, by focusing our vision, always leaves something out. Indeed, it leaves everything else out and makes it hard to revisit the question about what we really want. And subordinating our means to that end makes it hard to see when other, perhaps equally valuable, goods are being damaged in the pursuit of whatever we have chosen to focus on.

The first stipulation entails that we are in no position to try to give up or undo our predilection for increasing the rationalization of the means/ends relationships that structure our lives. The second entails that without the careful maintenance and deployment of a self-critical dimension to our means/ends thinking, it will inevitably eventuate in disaster. We will foul our nest, irremediably, in the process of perfecting it.

A survey of the vocabulary at work in discussions about higher education shows that means/ends thinking orthodoxy is at play. The passion for ensuring student outcomes speaks for itself: Are we achieving our aims? The impetus for efficiency is the question whether our means are the most economical and effective. Is what we are doing cost effective? Accountability is the question whether those charged with employing the means are doing their jobs well. Transparency is the issue whether we can make out what they're doing. The insistence on the primacy of so-called STEM disciplines—science, technology, engineering, and mathematics—is a commitment to certain educational ends as social and economic means toward further ends, perhaps employment, material progress, or national stature. The question about the worth of the liberal arts, especially the humanities and social sciences, is the question whether they have determinate ends—that is, whether they are means to anything worth having. If they aren't, in this vision, if they don't produce something, if they don't get us somewhere, then by the remorseless logic of this system, they are worthless.

It is important to see that the rationalization of means/ends relationships defines value. In a state of nature, we value whatever catches our fancy. We want something to eat and to gain shelter from the elements, certainly. But we also value a nice nap, loafing in the grass, chasing this or that will of the wisp, and simply celebrating idleness. Walt Whitman captured this admirably: "I loaf and invite my soul, / I lean and loaf at my ease observing a spear of summer grass."[10] Life is about being, about celebrating meaning. But this is not the spirit that produced indoor plumbing and paved roads, let alone iPads and iPhones. By structuring our lives and activities, the rationalization of means/ends relations also structures our perception, our values, and our of sense of reality.

Where do decisions about ends come from? Are ends simply "given"? Aristotle opined that there was no deliberating about ends, but only about means,[11] though philosophers have disagreed as to whether he could have really meant this to be universally true, since it would imply that ends are irrational and unshakeable. And he does imply elsewhere in the *Ethics* (in book 6) that we can and do deliberate about ends, even about the ultimate end, which he calls eudaemonia, usually translated as "happiness." It seems inevitable that such deliberation be possible. What if our end turned out to be impossible? Or contained contradictions? What if people disagree about which ends to pursue, as they certainly will?

The right conclusion, surely, is that it is necessary for a culture to maintain and exercise the self-critical capacity to reconsider and reevaluate its major ends. In order to do so, it will need to cultivate patterns of reflection that are, from the perspective of its dominant ends, trivial, beside the point, useless, and irrelevant. If such patterns of reflection could be justified in terms of the dominant ends, the reflections would not have the critical distance required to offer alternatives to the dominant ends.

As for means, if efficiency in achieving the desired end is the sole criterion for its adoption, how are we to tell whether such means might also involve unintended consequences we might not desire? What if they have some disastrous side effect? To detect and respond to such a side effect is to bring to bear a consideration outside the calculation of means and ends that led us to adopt the means in the first place. If killing midwestern milkweed endangers monarch butterflies, we have to move outside the considerations that led some of us to try to kill the milkweed. In a world of complex interrelationships, it seems impossible to know all that is entailed by our choices. And some things unintentionally entailed by our choices may well be things we would choose not to cause to happen.

So a culture, even when it agrees about the broad ends to be pursued, must maintain self-critical capacity to reconsider and reevaluate its major means. In order to do so it will need to cultivate sensitivity to the unintended effects of its means, considering things that are, from the perspective of the end for the sake of which they were adopted, irrelevant. In order to avoid unintentional self-destruction, then, a culture needs to cultivate reflection upon irrelevancies.

So we can question the desirability of ends and the suitability of means only if we are able to step outside the given structure and ask questions based on values and meanings that are ignored by it. It is this stepping outside of received opinions that can make deliberation seem unpredictable, threatening, and even chaotic. This suspension of the presumed rules of relevance opens issues up beyond the focus of our pursuit. This is how discussions of timber bring up owls, how pipelines bring up aquifers and sacred grounds, and how natural gas is related to drinking water. We can ignore these intrusions only if we are certain that our ends and choice of means already maximize the realization of every value we might hold. But to believe that we are ever justifiably certain of that is the stuff of tragedy.

2

WITTGENSTEIN ON RULES AND ITS RELEVANCE FOR LIBERAL EDUCATION

IT MAY SEEM ODD that one of the most influential philosophers of the twentieth century was also one of the most opaque. Ludwig Wittgenstein worried that others would say of his work, "I understand all he says, but what on earth is he driving at?" Or "I see what he's driving at, but how on earth is he going to get there?"[1] His concern was well founded. I remember my first encounter with his book *Philosophical Investigations*. I was on an intercity bus between Memphis and Little Rock. Riding through the utter darkness of the Arkansas delta, looking at pages of German facing English, I was unsure whether the deeper obscurity lay outside the bus or inside the text.

The book begins with a puzzling quotation from St. Augustine's *Confessions* about how a child learns the meanings of words, a quotation that, by the way, we are to come to understand as captivatingly wrong, but this conclusion is only hinted. Then we get a vignette about a man who goes to the grocer's with a slip of paper on which is written "five red apples." The grocer opens the drawer marked "apples," checks a color chart for the sample of red, and pulls out apples of the proper color as he recites the cardinal numbers up to five. Wittgenstein, in his authorial voice says, "It is in this and similar ways that one operates with words." His imagined interlocutor replies, "But how does he know where and how he is to look up the word 'red'?" Wittgenstein counters: "Well, I assume that he acts as I have described. Explanations come to an end somewhere" (*PI* 1). Another vignette features a pair of builders who call out instructions to one another using only monosyllabic nouns. We are asked to consider this a complete (though primitive) language. "What," I thought, "is going on here?" The bus stopped in the middle of nowhere and a man got on. He rode for several miles and then the bus stopped, and he got off in the dark.

That was nearly a half century ago. I have now a better idea of what Wittgenstein's work comes to. I have confidence that the effort required to understand it is richly repaid, but its relevance to departments of life beyond problems in logic and language requires some explanation. So this chapter will be largely Wittgenstein. The next will connect his thought with the central aim of education in the liberal arts and then consider the impact of that connection on several practical topics in liberal arts education.

I have begun by sowing doubt. Wittgenstein's life was not exemplary of the liberal arts. His family thought his talents were technical and mechanical. As a boy he built a working sewing machine. He was educated at home and then sent to the *Realgymnasium* in Linz, Austria, where Adolph Hitler was also a student, rather than to a classical *Gymnasium,* which would have prepared him for a university education. He hoped, briefly, to study with the brilliant Vienna engineering professor Ludwig Boltzmann. He became fascinated with the design of propellers for aircraft—then in their infancy—which plunged him into mathematics, then into the foundations of mathematics, then into problems of logic as presented in Bertrand Russell and Alfred North Whitehead's *Principia Mathematica.* When he became a student at Cambridge in 1912–13, that was a mere device for gaining access to Russell, at whose door he appeared with questions. "Am I a complete idiot," he asked, "because if I am, I will become an aeronaut. If not, I will become a philosopher." Russell, characteristically, told him he didn't know, and asked for an essay. Reading it, he told Wittgenstein, "You should not become an aeronaut."[2]

While he did become a philosopher, he largely shunned conventional teaching and conventional writing. The only book published in his lifetime saw print mostly through the efforts of others. He gardened at a monastery, taught elementary school, unsuccessfully, in the Austrian Alps, and even designed a house for his sister, in a spare Bauhaus style. He gave away the fortune he had inherited and lived a life of intentional poverty. Cambridge awarded him a PhD, based on his one book, which was already regarded as a classic, his examiners being Russell and the ethicist G. E. Moore. He became a professor but continued to spend months accumulating into years alone at a hut he built on a remote Norwegian fjord.

As a teacher he was terrifying. His seminars were occasions of spontaneous, original thinking, conducted with the class as a rapt, captive audience. Bringing their chairs in from the staircase landing, they were subjected to his silent mental struggles, punctuated with questions he answered himself and then rejected with exclamations about his own—as he said—stupidity. Students who ventured contributions were subjected to the same harsh treatment he gave himself. Russell called him "perhaps the most perfect example I have ever known of a genius as traditionally conceived—passionate, proud, intense, and dominating."[3]

He was devoid of conventional bonhomie, and even his closest friends felt the lash of his unrelenting judgment. Memoirs and biographies abound with stories of his behavior over a range from stiff awkwardness to gratuitous cruelty. He seemed incapable of ordinary small talk. Testimony of this incapacity is given by a central figure of the Bloomsbury set, Leonard Woolf, husband of the more famous Virginia Woolf.[4] Two examples will illustrate this tendency. He treated John Maynard Keynes's wife, Lydia, with what Leonard Woolf called "brutal rudeness."[5] David Edmonds and John Eidinow, authors of *Wittgenstein's Poker*, report that what happened was this: Lydia Lopokova made an appreciative remark about a tree: "'What a beautiful tree!' she exclaimed. Wittgenstein glared at her; 'What do you mean?' She burst into tears."[6] More famously, at a meeting of the Moral Science Club he seems to have threatened the philosopher Karl Popper, the guest of honor, with a fireplace poker.

The doubt I meant to sow is this: not only does Wittgenstein never formally discuss liberal arts, his life of struggle and torturing doubt seems far removed from the life of balance and steadiness we hold up as instantiating the liberally educated person. He was deeply interested in music, in cheap American detective novels, and American western movies, but they seem to have provided more escape than balance in his life. So there seems almost nothing in his life or philosophical work, or in his cultural milieu—the Vienna of the Hapsburg twilight—to suit him as a resource for thinking about the problems of understanding the value of the liberal arts.

And yet there is. It can be summed up in this statement by Matthew Bevis: "One of the problems with rules is that you need to know when and how to apply them. And there's no rule for that."[7] Wittgenstein's later work addresses just this problem. In order to get there, we need to look briefly at his earlier work, which grew in part from his encounters with Bertrand Russell.

WITTGENSTEIN'S EARLY VIEW OF LANGUAGE AND LOGIC

Wittgenstein's *Tractatus*, published in 1921, developed a starkly simple view of language and meaning, largely in response to a paradox that lay at the base of Russell and Whitehead's philosophy of mathematics. Known as "Russell's paradox," it can be formally stated in terms of set theory, or informally in this way: Consider a village containing among its population a barber who shaves all and only those who do not shave themselves. Does this barber shave himself? If he does shave himself, then he must not shave himself, and if he does not, then he must shave himself. Russell took this paradox seriously enough to develop a way around it, which he called the theory of types. The theory of types holds that things you may say about sets of things—for instance, the set of all University of Arkansas football players—you may not say about sets of sets, for instance, the set of all Southeastern Conference football teams. That will prevent you from asking about the set of all sets that are not members of themselves whether it is a member of itself. No set could possibly be a member of itself because the set for which it would be a candidate would be a set of a different type, or level. Wittgenstein spotted this as an obvious problem, because it requires you to know what type any set belongs to before you know what can be said or asked about it. Which makes logic contingent upon matters of fact.

Wittgenstein's solution—which may seem equally desperate—was to insist that logic cannot be expressed at all, but only displayed, or shown. This conclusion follows from a rigorously interrelated set of principles, beginning with the picture theory of the proposition. According to that theory, a proposition is an assemblage of names, standing for objects in the world. In the proposition the names are related in a certain logical way, meant to mirror the relation of the objects they represent. They *show* that relation in the way they stand, one to another, but it can't be *said;* that is, it can't be made explicit in language. That is because all propositions *say* the same thing, which is "Things in the world stand in the same relation to each other as we do to one another." So logic is both trivial and, at the same time and for the same reason, what makes language work. It's shown, not stated, and you just have to be able to see it.

The *Tractatus*'s theory of language falls under the rubric of logic, and is thus, by the book's own theory, nonsensical. Wittgenstein embraced this conclusion, saying that you had to pull the ladder up after yourself after using it to see the world aright and then insisting in the last line of the book that what you can't speak about, you must pass over in silence. Anything that can be said at all can be said clearly. According to this theory, only propositions about the facts of the world make sense, and everything else—talk about value, ethics, aesthetics, the self that limits the world at one edge and God at the other—is nonsense. At this point, believing himself to have solved "all the problems of philosophy," Wittgenstein abandoned the discipline. Aside from this book, he published only a brief essay on logic. But he labored continually at philosophy for decades and left behind at his death an enormous *Nachlass*, elaborating a very different resolution of "the problems of philosophy."

Between the wars, Wittgenstein lectured at Cambridge, and G. E. Moore, author of *Principia Ethica*, attended the lectures. In the notes Moore took, we find him baffled by Wittgenstein's thought processes as he probed the foundations of logic. Moore found him developing an account of logic and language based on systems of rules and common human agreement about how things are done. Wittgenstein, in those lectures, compared the foundations of logic to aesthetics, and according to Moore, insisted that the question of aesthetics was not "Do you like this?" But "*Why* do you like it?" That question, as I will argue in the next chapter, lies at the heart of the deliberative enterprise that is the focal aim of education in the liberal arts.

LANGUAGE GAMES

Language, as envisioned in the *Tractatus*, does not require a speaker; the self lies outside the world as an observer. In the *Investigations*, central to the later view, the speaker is embodied in the world. The speakers of languages take part in activities; those activities are intrinsically social, the learning of language takes place as an element of participation in those activities, and the activities are innumerable because characterizing something as a "language-game"—Wittgenstein's term of art—can be done from a variety of perspectives depending on the point we are trying to make. You could consider calls made in sports by officials a language game, or calls made in baseball, or calls made by home plate umpires, or strike calls made by home plate umpires; any of these would qualify, depending on what you are trying to make clear about how the activity goes.

In fact, he exploits the richness of the concept "game" in a variety of ways. Sometimes he deploys the term to designate a simple way of working with words in order to make some point. Sometimes "language games" are the actual practices children engage in when they are learning to speak. Sometimes the term is used to emphasize that the use of language is always a case of *doing something.* And sometimes Wittgenstein uses the variety of games themselves—from board games to organized sports to children's games like hopscotch—to illustrate the fact that a concept's utility need not depend on shared features.

Such language games resemble each other more or less—Wittgenstein uses the term "family resemblance" to make the point that not all kinds of language use will possess all the features common among them. Some branches of the family have features not shared elsewhere—the "play on" call in soccer, for instance. All, presumably, are related to what's happening in the game—except for the call "play ball," which must precede anything happening in the game. All have presuppositions which are the conditions of their making sense. An umpire can't stand alone at the plate in the dark of night and cry out "play ball" and create a ball game. To whom is he talking? What is he even *doing*? But sharing enough features will allow us to mark out "language," though it won't rule out or decide borderline cases.

Wittgenstein concluded that problems about the meanings of words were to be resolved by coming to clarity about their *use,* a principle embedded in the slogan "meaning is use." But that doesn't mean that the use of a word is some *thing.* Not all nouns—this is another departure from the *Tractatus*—name things. So if the meanings of words are their uses in language games, where is the stability that makes logic logic? Words can be used in different ways; they can change meanings; they can even be used to mean the opposite of what they "mean." How can we make sense of anything in this chaotic view?

(At this point I think of Blaise Pascal's sensing the void opening beside his reading chair,[8] of David Hume's conclusion that there can be no reasoned expectation that the future will resemble the past,[9] and of Robert Pirsig's narrator in *Zen and the Art of Motorcycle Maintenance,*[10] who confronted the epistemological ineffable at the cost of his sanity.)

Whereas in the *Tractatus* Wittgenstein wrote that he had resolved the problems of philosophy (all of them), in his later view, there is no final resolution of the problems of philosophy, because the ways of language are so many and various, and they are always giving rise to new confusions. One of the earliest points made in *Philosophical Investigations* is that language is endlessly various. "But how many kinds of sentence are there? . . . There are countless kinds. . . . And this multiplicity is not something fixed. . . . But new types of language . . . Come into existence and others become obsolete and get forgotten" (*PI* §23). He invites the reader to consider the variety of things we regard as "description" (*PI* §24) and lists exclamations that work in different ways to illustrate how different their uses are.

ESCAPE FROM THE IDEAL

Wittgenstein's discussion of rules in *Philosophical Investigations* (§80–242) is really the heart of the argument. The concept of games provides entrée into the concept of rule following (*PI* §54), and it turns out that there is a wide array of roles that rules can play in governing games. For example, suppose I leave the children with you, instructing you to teach them a game, and come back to discover that you are teaching them poker. "That's not what I meant, I say." Well, isn't poker a game? How did I not mean poker?

When I understand a rule, its meaning seems to hit me "in a flash," but how can all future uses of the rule be prescribed in that instant? The rule guides me as I make moves in the game. Is there a characteristic feeling of "being guided"? And what are we to say of the tension between the "inner sense" of what the rule commands and my following it "automatically" once I've become habituated to it?

All these questions are colored by what Wittgenstein calls "misunderstanding of the role of the ideal in our language." "The ideal" here is that sense of absoluteness and precision, of perfect order, possessed by our concept of logic, the force of the logical "must." "The ideal" is what Lewis Carroll's Achilles referred to when he said to the Tortoise, "Logic would take you by the throat, and force you to accept [the conclusion]. . . . You can't help yourself. . . . So, you've no choice, you see."[11]

Wittgenstein's response is simple. He points out that the crystalline purity of logic was "not a *result of investigation:* it was a requirement." It's like slippery ice where, lacking friction, we are unable to walk. He writes: "We want to walk: so we need *friction:* Back to the rough ground!" (*PI* §107).

That is, back to ordinary language, back to real life, back to cases and actual confusions. We need to remove the idea of crystalline purity (*PI* §108) and turn our examination around and look at the real world. We need to realize that when one is "tracing the outline of a thing's nature over and over again, one is merely tracing round the frame through which we look at it" (*PI* §114). He follows this observation up by noting of his theory of the proposition in the *Tractatus:* "A *picture* held us captive" (*PI* §115).

AGREEMENT AND MEASUREMENT

Let's begin wresting away from that captivity by considering that "the word 'agreement' and the word 'rule' are *related* to one another, they are cousins. If I teach anyone the use of the one word, he learns the use of the other with it" (*PI* §224). That means that teaching someone a rule is teaching him or her to agree under what circumstances the rule should be said to have been followed. And instructing someone when to agree the rule has been followed is teaching him or her the rule. That means following a rule is a practice, a custom, an institution (*PI* §202). It is necessarily public and social, and it is grounded in learning a technique. As Wittgenstein wrote, "If language is to be a means of communication there must be agreement not only in definitions, but also . . . in judgments. . . . What we call measuring is partly determined by a certain constancy in results of measuring" (*PI* §242).

Consider a form of measurement that clearly lacks such constancy: the calling of balls and strikes in baseball. The very vocabulary of the game embodies the imprecision of the measurement. A ball can "paint the corner" of the plate, or "catch the black." The zone can expand or shrink. A television screen can offer more apparent precision with a superimposed box, but then we have to accept the accuracy of its dimensions and placement and the positioning of the dots that represent pitches. At some point, if there is to be a game, we have to accept what the umpire says. In the old story, the base runner looks up from his slide at the umpire and asks, "What am I?" The umpire replies: "You ain't nothin' till I say so." Even outside of formal games like baseball, there is remarkable human ability to agree on the results of measurement and thus, broadly, on the meanings of words and thus to communicate.

Someone might object: "Calling balls and strikes is a matter of judgment. We can always make things precise by measurement." Consider the question, "How long is the coastline of Britain?" According to the British Ordnance Survey, cited in the Wikipedia article "The Coast Line of the United Kingdom," it's 11,072.76 miles—a very precise answer that takes it down to hundredths of a mile, or 52.80 feet. But quite possibly not very accurate. If you add larger islands to the coastline, as measured by the standard method at Mean High Water Mark, it's 19,491 miles. The CIA *Factbook* gives the number as 7,723 miles, though the CIA *Factbook* discloses nothing about how this figure is determined. The British Cartographic Society wisely says that the true answer is, "It depends." What it depends on is principally the scale of the unit of measurement used in measuring the coastline. And because the coastline is fractal in nature, meaning that it replicates the same features at every stage of magnification, it will resist every attempt to supply an absolute answer.

The reality is indeterminate and can be represented in our knowledge only approximately. Worse, decisions will have to be made about whether to include tidal pools, what to say about tidal changes more broadly, what to say about the incessant wearing away and building up of coastline. What this means is that the coastline of Britain *can* be measured more or less precisely, but there is no such thing as the length it actually is. In *Investigations* Wittgenstein considers the concept of "exactness," concluding that "'inexact' is really a reproach, and 'exact' is praise. And that is to say that what is inexact attains its goal less perfectly than what is more exact. And thus the point here is what we call goal'" (*PI* §88). At some point we will need to ask why we want to know and how close is good enough.

All this reminds me of a question in Robert J. Fogelin's *Evidence and Meaning*. The sun and the moon appear to be about the same size in the sky, even though the sun is enormously larger in fact. The sun appears to be no bigger than the moon because it is so far way. So how close to the sun would you have to be to see it as big as it really is? The size the sun really is will always be relative to some system of measurement, which may be more or less coarse- or fine-grained. Of course, there is a perfectly suitable answer to the question. To see the sun as the size it really is, relative to the moon, you need to look at it from the same distance as the moon. And saying that rests the idea of objective comparison squarely on relativism.

THE IMPLICIT UNDERPINNINGS OF RULE-FOLLOWING

Recognizing the idea of an absolute precision as an imposition of our inquiry rather than a feature of the thing being investigated will allow us to recognize how it is that instructions that appear quite vague can be perfectly adequate. Consider a recipe that instructs us to "blend in two eggs." What do these instructions assume we know? That, unless instructed otherwise, we are to use hen's eggs, that we are to choose eggs that have not previously been cooked, that the eggs in question shall not have "gone bad," that we should crack the shells and discard them, using only their contents and not the other way around, that unless instructed otherwise we should use both parts of the inside of the eggs, and so on. They assume we know what "blend" means. Notice that knowing when eggs have "gone bad" is a judgment call—sometimes an obvious one, and cracking eggs is a technique—or a family of them. Furthermore, following a recipe like this is not something you learn all at once. You learn it by observing, imitating, succeeding and failing, and ultimately mastering it.

We are trained to follow rules that are expressed with the degree of precision and explicitness required for ordinary cases. As Wittgenstein remarks, a vague instruction may be perfectly adequate: "Stand roughly there," accompanied by a hand wave (*PI* §88). And how did we learn what the hand wave means? The human gestural repertoire is dangerous ground for generalization; while some gestures seem near universal (raised eyebrows are a signal of receptivity to further communication on the streets of Macon, Georgia, and in remote New Guinea highlands), others are not (think of the various hand gestures that are friendly in some cultures, obscenely insulting in others, and meaningless in still others).

We can even overcome paradox in finding the meaning of instructions. Everyone has seen the signs that say, "No Parking Between Signs." You know that these signs hunt in pairs. What they mean is "No Parking Between This Sign and the Other Sign That Also Says No Parking Between Signs." But *which* other sign that also says "No Parking Between Signs"?

Well, clearly, the nearest and most obvious. So our judgments are called on to determine which among all the No Parking Between Signs signs are nearest and most obvious. And each sign needs to be paired with that other one, and so each needs to read "No Parking Between This Sign and the Nearest and Most Obvious Sign That Also Says No Parking Between This Sign and the Nearest and Most Obvious Sign that Also Says. . . ." And so forth, bouncing from the first sign to the second back to the first, unendingly. But we are not confused. We just look around and find the sign.

In a similar fashion we are not prevented by Zeno's Paradox from reaching our destination. Remember that Zeno's Paradox says that you cannot cross a finish line because the space between you and that finish line can be divided into infinitely many smaller spaces, each of which must require at least some time to cross. But we step across that infinity of spaces every day. In the same way we are not lured into endless shampooing by the instructions on the shampoo bottle that read "Wash, rinse, repeat"—a clear, apparently irresistible invitation into what Douglas Hofstadter, the author of *Gödel, Escher, Bach,* called a "strange loop." We are rescued from logic by the exigencies of everyday life. Where rules are, so to speak, incomplete, we operate successfully when we "get it." Here is an acknowledgment of "getting it" from an online recipe in which the cook describes her grandmother's behavior: "She gave me her recipe from memory. Telling me about her tips as she went. . . . She told how she supposed someone had measured it out sometime, but she just added the flour until it looked right. I could see the dough change and could feel the consistency of the mixture at each step. There is some information you can't get from books."[12]

My own grandmother made biscuits the same way, never measuring, working in the shortening in a big pan of flour, pouring buttermilk until the dough felt right, and then pulling out the wad of dough and putting away the pan, still full of dry flour.

REGRESS OF EXPLANATIONS

It is a mistake to suppose that every conceivable misunderstanding must be met with a rule that clarifies the first rule and rules out the misunderstanding. That way lies infinite regress, as Wittgenstein shows: "No course of action could be determined by a rule, because every course of action could be made out to accord with the rule" on some interpretation (*PI* §201). So if we always need another interpretation to clarify the rule, there is no such thing as following a rule. "What this shows," writes Wittgenstein, "is there is a way of grasping a rule which is *not an interpretation*."

Consider that bags of ice—the kind you buy at the grocery store—typically bear this admonition: "Keep frozen!" Well, ice typically melts when you use it for its intended purpose. You have to "get it" that you willfully disobey this order at the right time. Rules are good enough, clear enough, when people can be guided by them—when people "get" them. Wittgenstein writes in *On Certainty,* "Not only rules, but also examples are needed for establishing a practice. Our rules leave loopholes open, and the practice has to speak for itself."[13]

In a similar way, doubt requires a reason. Descartes's project of calling everything into doubt can be seen to be a nonstarter by considering what would have happened had he called into doubt whether he understood French. That would be like saying, "What I am now saying may make no sense at all. I just can't tell." Where do you go from there, in an unreliable language? Anything can be brought into question, but not everything all at once.

Free-floating, groundless expressions of doubt are not genuine doubts. Genuine doubts occur in systems that can offer means for resolving them. Wittgenstein called such systems "world pictures," or *Weltbilder.* And these rely ultimately on forms of behavior that are neither justified by reasons nor unjustified because they lack reasons. "The squirrel does not infer by induction that it is going to need stores for next winter," Wittgenstein observes (*OC* §287). He calls the basis of language games "something animal" (*OC* §358).

HOW THINGS STRIKE US

It is important that these certainties are not—so to speak—considered conclusions based on reflection. They are how things strike us, what we take things for, not what—after weighing things up—we *decide* that things mean. There is no act of decision. Agreements in judgment are the ground of meaning. Perhaps ironically, Wittgenstein says very little about these forms of life. He says that they constitute the "inherited background against which I distinguish between true and false" (*OC* §94). He writes: "A language-game does not have its origin in *consideration*."[14] The propositions that describe this background are not, typically, explicitly learned or taught, but they come along implicitly as we learn to do things. Think of someone's confidence that the earth existed for a long, long time before his birth and will exist after his death.

These propositions compose a "world picture," and they are as fixed as anything could be. But it is important that there is a certain fluidity in this background. Some propositions, as it were, are hardened, and function as channels for the rest, but, Wittgenstein says, this relation can alter with time: "In that fluid propositions hardened, and hard ones became fluid" (*OC* §96). There is a stretch in the notes published as *On Certainty* where Wittgenstein anticipates in outline the view of Thomas Kuhn in *The Structure of Scientific Revolutions* concerning "normal science" and "paradigm shifts," sharing with Kuhn the view that such shifts are not fully explicable in rational terms (*OC* §94–99). This is because paradigms condition what counts as rational, as do world pictures.

As in *Philosophical Investigations* Wittgenstein noted that the concept of measurement depends on a certain constancy in the results of measurement, and in our general agreement about those results, so in the notes published as *Zettel* he says that the acquisition of color words, words like red, blue, green, and so on, depends on general agreement about their applicability (*Z* §429). And he makes the point that if we did not agree about that, it's not that the language game with colors *would* not exist; it *could* not exist (*Z* §506).

Consider the case of the pointing arrow on a sign. The arrow points in a direction indicated by an abstract representation of the arrow's "head": →. We accept this partly because we grew up in a culture whose history included actual arrows. But suppose we had not and had grown up instead in a culture familiar with certain shore birds whose tracks looked like this: →. And from that track there had evolved the accepted use of the same symbol (→) used to indicate direction by mimicking the direction of the bird's walk in the sand. It would "point" in the opposite direction. What this shows is the arbitrariness of symbols and their reliance on cultural histories.

We should not expect this way of seeing things to advance in our understanding point by point, as it were, gaining ground like yardage in football. Rather, as Wittgenstein writes, dawn breaks slowly over the whole, as things become more and more visible for what they are. Things come into focus gradually. And the *slow* cure, he writes, is all important (*Z* §382). That is because the problems that beset our thinking keep cropping up and confusing us all over again. That means, as Wittgenstein writes, again in *Zettel,* that philosophical work has no end. It has no end because it is piecemeal, straightening out misunderstandings as they come along and cause problems. From the book of *Job* (5:7): "Man is born unto trouble, as the sparks fly upward." "Trouble" here is disagreement. In *Zettel* Wittgenstein writes of the expectation of uniformity of behavior: "But where I am *certain,* someone else is uncertain. And that is a fact of nature" (*Z* §374).

SUMMARY

Let me summarize this discussion of rule following. It is in the nature of rules that they invite infinite regress when the attempt is made to make them fully explicit and to guard them against every conceivable misunderstanding or misconstrual. Yet since rules do work, for the most part, there must be a way of following a rule that is not supplying another rule. That way consists in the practice or custom, a way of following the rule that rests on how people respond to certain facts, gestures, and other accompaniments of speech and on their being trained in the use of words in the course of learning to do something. We acquire such customs or practices by being trained into them. Successful training is grounded in forms of life that blend our natural reactions, aptitudes, and inclinations with arbitrary decisions, and only in that context can we "get it." In this process there is continuity of the aesthetic with the ethical and with the "cognitive."

Exemplars, or classic cases of a rule's having been rightly applied, are necessary for this learning. When people disagree about whether a rule has been followed, they are disagreeing about which purported exemplars are, in fact, exemplary. To come to agreement about whether a rule has been followed is to accept the same exemplars in the same ways.

A variety of things may count as following a rule. It is in principle impossible to find a rule that explicitly binds every conceivable case. Rules typically lack sharp boundaries of application. Reasons explaining how a rule is to be applied cannot go on forever. So following a rule is a practice, or a custom.

There can be no completely explicit account of the meaning of a rule. Anything can count as being in accord with a rule, or violating it, on some interpretation. (Another rule.) Thus there has to be a way of following a rule that is *not* another rule. That way is found in practice, not reasoning. (This is the point of taming exactness.) How do we learn rules? Through training in a practice. What is training? Seeking agreement that the rule has been followed. What are the grounds of agreement? (1) Taking for and seeing as—natural human reactions and capacities. (This sounds something like naturalism.) (2) Acculturation. (This sounds something like social relativism.) (3) Stipulation. (This sounds arbitrary.). Put all together, it sounds something like pragmatism. Wittgenstein recognized that fact and repudiated it. Why?

It is self-defeating to attempt to construct a fully explicit account—a rule—about how we operate with rules, in the face of the fact that fully explicit accounts will always be unavailable. The attempt will end in the regressive paradox of supplying further rules or in the paradox of indeterminacy in which everything and nothing satisfies the rule. The message is to look at actual cases and you'll see how, for that rule and in that case, the rule is followed. Remember, this is philosophy that eschews the final, settled conclusion that fits every imaginable case.

RELEVANCE TO LIBERAL ARTS EDUCATION

It is now possible to make clear the claim that Wittgenstein's work bears a direct relation to the aims of liberal education. Wittgenstein's aim was not to establish particular truths, especially not purportedly foundational truths. He did not aim to build an edifice of knowledge. Rather, he sought to advance a certain way of seeing language, knowledge, and the world, a way that eschews the enthronement of the ideal, crystalline view of logic and instead immerses itself in the actual use of language. It is a way of seeing things that frankly acknowledges the reliance of formalized systems on their unformalized underpinnings and therefore sees that there are limits—indeed, pitfalls—in overreliance on them.

More acutely, Wittgenstein held that overreliance on formalized systems was a cause of much of the confusion that bedevils us and had to be struggled against. The unformalized underpinnings to which he brought attention were a jumble of factors. Sometimes sheer contingency is at work, as in the meaning of the word "wan," which once meant "swarthy" and now means "pale." Sometimes very general facts about the world and our place in it are in play, such as the fact that almost no one has been very far from the surface of the earth. But most strikingly, the underpinnings consist of very general, though not necessarily universal, facts about how people react to certain stimuli, how they can distinguish between a friendly greeting and a threat, how some music sounds sad and other music sounds joyous, how most of us can distinguish a red light from a green one, and on and on. There is little point in attempting to formalize this enormous range of skills and capacities. But there may be much utility in adducing one or another in relieving us of a philosophical quandary.

In the notes published as *Zettel* and *On Certainty,* Wittgenstein considers various ways in which concepts different from our familiar ones could be formed. Could there be people who don't command the form of words "I was just going to say" and we haven't noticed them (*Z* §143)? Or people who make mistakes in calculating so regularly that they literally could not "check their work" by repeating it (*Z* §393)? Language games are an extension of unlearned, "primitive" behaviors (*Z* §545), and yet Wittgenstein expresses dissatisfaction at the characterization of such behaviors as "forms of life": he means ways of behaving that are "something that lies beyond being justified or unjustified; as it were, as something animal" (*OC* §358).

And yet specifying forms of life in justification of a practice, making it "right" or "correct," always also involves culture, education, instruction, and what we could call "training." Wittgenstein's word is "*Abrichtung,*" a word that can imply habituation in a practice through repetition, the way children learn the alphabet or multiplication tables. He writes: "An education quite different from ours might also be the foundation for quite different concepts" (*Z* §387). So the structural elements of our picture of the world are not inevitable. Alternatives are, at the very least, imaginable.

Wittgenstein writes of "persuasion" as the method of communicating between adherents of different world pictures. Liberal education is the gaining of the capacity to explore this zone of examining one's own acceptance of exemplars: one's predilections, habits, preferences, "natural" tendencies, prejudices, blind spots, etc., and the acceptance of the endlessness of the task of self-examination thus presented.

The point of the quest for the Holy Grail is not that we achieve a grasp of the true grail. It's more like keeping up the quest. It's illustrated in the scene in *Monty Python and the Holy Grail* in which King Arthur is in conversation with a French knight on the battlements of a castle. Arthur asks the knight to convey to his master his invitation to join with him in his quest for the Holy Grail. The knight responds: "OK, I'll tell him. But I don't think he'll be very keen to go. You see, he's already got one." "Already got one?" says the startled Arthur. "Oh, yes," says the knight. "It's very nice!" The joke is complete, but now it gets a dash of lagniappe. Arthur says, "Do you think we could come up and have a look?" It is important to be willing to consider the other person's conception of the grail.

3

BENEFITS OF LIBERAL EDUCATION

Deliberation and the Emergence of Meaning

IN THE OPENING CHAPTER I gave an account of Ludwig Wittgenstein's project of reorienting our approach to philosophical problems, an account that involved coming to grips with a cluster of interrelated aspects of his thought. As I described in chapter 2, among that cluster are the following:

- the baleful role of the ideal in our thinking about language,
- the necessity of regarding language as an activity—a public, social family of undertakings with an innumerable complexity of purposes and functions, and
- the need to come to terms with the facts about how language emerges from primitive, untaught behaviors and never loses its dependence on them.

In chapter 2 I also extended the exploration of Wittgenstein's project, especially his conclusions about

- the role of contingent, nonnecessary agreements in providing the basis for our ability to follow rules;
- the role that training (*Abrichtung*) plays in laying the groundwork for understanding and the role played by "getting it," or "catching on" in our endeavors; and
- therefore, the necessity that explanations—giving reasons—has to come to an end somewhere.

All that Wittgenstein claimed about language and rule following should inspire us to reconsider the usual ways of thinking about the definition, skills, aims, and benefits of liberal education. The work of this chapter is to make this Wittgensteinian approach to the liberal arts more compellingly evident. I will contend that the capacity to deliberate, with all its extensive intellectual and moral dexterities, is the central skill of the liberal arts, and the chief aim is disciplined reflection on the emergence of meaning.

WHAT ARE THE BENEFITS OF LIBERAL EDUCATION?

The preface to Wittgenstein's *Philosophical Investigations* is spot-on at this point, so I will quote it at some length. His work, he writes,

> compels us to travel over a wide field of thought criss-cross in every direction.—The philosophical remarks in this book are, as it were, a number of sketches of landscapes

> which were made in the course of these long and involved journeyings.
>
> The same or almost the same points were always being approached afresh from different directions, and new sketches made. (*PI* ix)

In the spirit of this metaphor, in this chapter I will, so to speak, circle around the perimeter of our topic—the liberal arts—and come at the question from a very different angle.

A number of questions could frame the fresh approach to this topic. What is the value of the arts and sciences? Why should anyone study liberal arts? What does liberal education prepare you to do? Underlying, or commingled with, these questions are others, like, What are the liberal arts, anyway? Is there an essential content to liberal education, or is it all about the style of education?

People have been offering answers to these and similar questions at least since the time of Socrates, so I don't think it possible or plausible to claim to have found the "right" way of framing and pursuing them. But it may be possible to offer one plausible account, based on some (admittedly nonscientific) evidence, that has some direct relevance to pressing issues in the contemporary world. That's my intention.

Leaving aside questions of defining the liberal arts, let's think for a moment about what the defenders of arts and sciences claim for them. Often liberal education is contrasted with specialized, vocational, or professional education: education that prepares the student for a specific job. By contrast, liberal education is "broad," a metaphor often cashed out through distribution requirements that assure at least a little exposure to a variety of different disciplines or subject matters. We might ask why this is thought to be a good thing. I know of no magic that prevents well-informed people from being well-informed bores or well-informed boors. But there it is, like the inscription on the statue of the founder of *Animal House*'s Faber College: "Knowledge Is Good."

Samuel Johnson said that "knowledge is of two kinds. We know a subject ourselves, or we know where we can find information upon it."[1] Certainly, there is much to be said for the second kind of knowledge. But in a world in which we all carry around libraries in our pockets, it would be easy to devalue the first kind—simply knowing a lot. Why bother, when you can always look it up? Well, when do we "look it up"? We look it up when we have occasion to—that is, when it becomes pertinent, relevant, valuable to know in the first sense. What are such occasions like? They arise when something we know only in the second sense connects with something we already know in the first sense. So the more you know something in the first sense—that is, the greater your command of the facts—the more such occasions will arise. Conversely, the lesser your command, the fewer such occasions. If you don't know there's a color called "puce," you can't wonder what the difference is between puce and mauve. If you don't know about house finches, you won't wonder about their difference from purple finches. And so on into things that matter.

To take one especially egregious example, a report from the National Constitution Center details the enormous gaps in public understanding of the authority and function of the third branch of our government.[2] Is the country no worse off that two-thirds of voters can't name a single justice of the Supreme Court, since they could always look it up? I don't think so. If you don't know who the justices are, you are unlikely to have informed views about their judicial philosophies, their voting records, or anything else about the court. Real knowledge is important. And we have to come to terms with what it should be, time and the curriculum being finite.

This problem is made acute by the fact that expanding knowledge is like an expanding balloon. The more it grows, the greater its surface area; that is, the more it comes into contact with the unknown. The more you know, the more you come into contact with what you don't know, and unlike a real balloon, which will burst at some point, the growth of knowledge is potentially infinite. So choices have to be made. I will return to this point in chapter 4, with recommendations based on decades of immersion in liberal education. But first, an important caveat.

Real knowledge is knowledge of the facts. But haven't we shown that there are no *real* facts, everything being relative? Yes and no. Yes, every claim to fact is relative to human perception and, more finely, relative to some conceptual system based on doing something. Facts are always situated in some matrix of common agreement. But within such matrices facts can be perfectly objective. Here is Michael Hayden, former director of the Central Intelligence Agency, expressing this thought: "Intelligence agencies are in the bunker with some unlikely mates: journalism, academics, the courts, law enforcement and science—all of which, like intelligence gathering, are evidence-based. Intelligence gathering shares a broader duty with these other truth-tellers to preserve the commitment and ability of our society to base important decisions on our best judgment of what constitutes objective reality."[3]

Hayden goes on to cite historian Timothy Snyder, who links our possession of facts with the possession of freedom and the resistance of unjust power: "If nothing is true, then no one can criticize power because there is no basis on which to do so." It is thus unutterably important not to follow the slippery slope of supposing that because anything can be called into question, everything can be called into question. That way lies nonsense and the reign of unfettered power for its own sake.

Often the argument is made that in addition to being well informed, or even quite apart from it, liberally educated people possess a repertoire of generally applicable skills and capacities that distinguish them as fit for a wide variety of roles in later life. One version of this view was supplied in 1914 to the entering class at Oxford by professor of moral philosophy John Alexander Smith: "Gentlemen, you are now about to embark on a course of studies that [will] form a noble adventure. . . . Let me make this clear to you. . . . Nothing that you will learn in the course of your studies will be of the slightest possible use to you in after life—save only this—that if you work hard and intelligently, *you should be able to detect when a man is talking rot,* and that, in my view, is the main, if not the sole purpose of education."

A more contemporary and comprehensive list of such skills might include higher forms of literacy, analytical skills, synthetic abilities, skills of detecting fallacies, and so on, including the capacity and inclination to continue learning throughout one's life. I will confess that I myself once thought that this was the entire point of liberal education. And so I claimed that I could teach an entirely adequate "Introduction to Philosophy" using as the text for the course the owner's manual to a toaster oven. While that was wild hyperbole, there is merit in the idea that the liberal arts can imbue skills and capacities that are widely applicable, generalizable, across many fields.

George Eliot writes, "It has been well said that the highest aim in education is analogous to the highest aim in mathematics, namely, to obtain not results but powers, not particular solutions but the means by which endless solutions may be wrought."[4]

This contention has been challenged with the claim that to be of value, learning must correlate with preparation for a specific job or profession. Let me offer for your entertainment a spirited rebuttal of that challenge:

> This is an intensely utilitarian age, and men virtually worship the "money-god" and will not cease until they are convinced that there are nobler and purer shrines at which to worship. . . . While we recognize in the bustling activity all around us the necessity for practical education, we do not pander to that depraved, money-born cry, "Nothing but the practical!" That education which, ignoring culture, burdens the student's mind with tables and technical terms, simply because these may be of use to him in his business or profession, is not practical but injurious in the extreme. The education founded upon what is best in Science and Literature, giving development to mind and heart, building strong by building deep and broad, is truly practical. The student who has learned to think, not merely to memorize, who has secured permanent culture and wisdom, who has absorbed and assimilated, but has not been stuffed and gorged, is the one who will be felt, wherever he may be.

This is likely the work of A. C. Millar, an early president of Hendrix College, and appears in the college's *Catalogue* for the 1890–91 academic year. We may perhaps forgive Millar for his assumption that the students are male, given the times. And we find, in Millar's account, elements that can be pulled together into a coherent picture: depth, breadth, absorption, and assimilation as opposed to being stuffed, thinking as opposed to memorizing, and developing both mind and heart—a reference to unifying the acquisition of factual knowledge and the structuring of values.

Another apologia for liberal education is that it is essential to the life and culture of a democratic society, that the liberal arts are the incubators of citizenship, even the guardians of human rights and freedoms. When Aristotle defined humanity as a political animal, he meant that humans are by nature fitted to live and flourish in communities. And it became important to define and cultivate the virtues that fit this life. The claim attributed to the Sophists, that they offered instruction to prepare citizens to perform well in public speaking, is a version of the same impulse.

Still another account of the value of the liberal arts holds that it is intrinsic, and that any attempt to explain their value by offering practical utility misses the point and may well degrade and devalue them. Stanley Fish has offered a version of this defense in his 2012 book, *Save the World on Your Own Time*, as has Helen Small, in the 2013 book *The Value of the Humanities*. There are others. The argument—if it is one—is similar to the remark that Rat makes to Mole in Kenneth Grahame's *The Wind in the Willows:* "Believe me, my young friend, there is *nothing*—absolutely nothing—half so much worth doing as simply messing about in boats."[5] There's nothing half so much worth doing as simply reflecting on the emergence of meaning, and any attempt to prove that such activities are worthwhile will beg the question by appealing to the emergence of meaning somewhere. It just is the case, on this argument, that immersing oneself in learning is—with all the proper caveats about balance and a life well lived—a good thing. If studying Shakespeare is not of and in itself a good thing, it is hard to know what pleasure or utility it could conduce to that would prove its instrumental value. The beauties of liberal arts are unique gems, not fungible banknotes.

As I said, this really isn't an argument, but it does capture the attitude of many who devote their lives to these studies and many of those who divert what time they can to them. I have a friend who, when he was practicing law, found himself getting up at 4:00 a.m. to read Spinoza, and not because he was going to be quoting the *Ethics* in a brief. It's also the spirit of a question asked by the warden of Rhodes House of Rhodes Scholars about to "go down": "Have you wasted enough time in Oxford?" That allusion to the fact that the best part of education is imparted by one's peers over coffee or beer was cheeky self-mockery from Sir Edgar Williams, who'd been Bernard Montgomery's chief of intelligence in North Africa.

More arguments and nonarguments for the value of liberal arts could be produced. But over a decade ago, Phi Beta Kappa decided to explore this issue by asking our old members to think about this question: "What has been of most lasting value in your education in the liberal arts?" We commissioned seventeen groups around the country and trained a group of moderators, using the people who train faculty for St. John's College in Annapolis—the "Great Books" college. The groups were provided with relevant reading material. They met for day-long sessions, and the trained reporters sent summaries of the conclusions to the national office of Phi Beta Kappa. We sent the summaries to David Alexander—then president of Pomona College and former American secretary to the Rhodes Scholarship Trust—for analysis.

The benefits I have already enumerated appeared in the accounts, along with a dominant theme that knits them all together. Of most lasting benefit, said these beneficiaries of liberal education, was the development of the skills of deliberation and the acquisition of the inclination to engage in it. Which raises the question, "What is deliberation?"

WHAT IS DELIBERATION?

I will approach this question through a contrast between the concept of deliberation and the concept of argument. The locus classicus for a discussion of the concept of argument is the famous "Argument Clinic" skit of Monty Python. In that skit, a man has entered an establishment where, for a fee, he can get a private room where someone will argue with him. After an initial miscue in a room designated for abuse, the following exchange begins the argument:

MAN: Ah, Is this the right room for an argument?

MR. VIBRATING: I told you once.

MAN: No you haven't.

MR. VIBRATING: Yes I have.

This exchange continues for a ridiculously long while, almost verbatim, until the man says,

MAN: Oh look, this isn't an argument.

MR. VIBRATING: Yes it is.

MAN: No it isn't. It's just contradiction.

MR. VIBRATING: No it isn't.

The argument then continues as to whether an argument *is* just contradiction.

> **MAN:** An argument isn't just contradiction.
>
> **MR. VIBRATING:** It can be.
>
> **MAN:** No it can't. An argument is a connected series of statements intended to establish a proposition.
>
> **MR. VIBRATING:** No it isn't.[6]

Imbedded in this lunacy is a pretty decent definition of what an argument is, apparently drawn from the *OED:* "An argument is a connected series of statements intended to establish a definite proposition." That's what we're looking for. An argument, in the philosophical sense, isn't just two people contradicting each other. It's an activity with an end in view, namely, the establishment of a proposition, and it consists in the presentation of a connected series of statements intended to accomplish that end.

How, we might ask, can a series of statements establish a proposition? Note that we are back to what Achilles said to the Tortoise. If all men are mortal and Socrates is a man, then that establishes that Socrates is mortal. And if you don't accept that, logic will come and take you by the neck and make you accept it! Except that's never going to happen. So let's back away from the ideal and note that those two statements, we would agree, offer good grounds for thinking that Socrates is mortal. They are relevant to the issue.

But the statements also need to be true. Let's ask what truth has to do with it. Paul Grice, an Englishman who did important work at Berkeley in the middle of the last century, developed four principles of conversational procedure. They are conventions implicitly and generally, though not universally, observed by people who are trying to communicate. The first he called "the principle of quality." This is the principle that, generally speaking, people tell the truth; reciprocally, people expect to have the truth told *to* them. Informal confirmations of this principle abound. The boy who falsely cries "Wolf!" is soon disbelieved. If I make a comment that is generally recognizable as obviously false, you assume I intend to convey the opposite: I am being sarcastic, or ironic. The principle of quality actually has two parts: (1) don't assert what you believe to be false (don't lie), and (2) don't assert propositions for which you lack adequate evidence (don't talk off the top of your head).

Grice's second principle is one of quantity. Make your contribution to the conversation appropriate in scope to the purposes of the conversation. This is a Goldilocks maxim: don't say too much and don't say too little. Make your contribution "just right." Of course people can differ about the purposes of a conversation they are having; one person's aim may be discovery and the other's obfuscation.

For that reason this principle bleeds into a third, the principle of relevance. In general, we expect what a person says to be relevant to the conversation's topic; that this is true is evidenced by the struggles we make to connect up to the topic at hand an apparently random remark someone might offer and the sternness with which we might say, "Don't change the subject!"

Finally, there is a principle of convenience, which encompasses using a language you expect your interlocutor to understand, not shouting or speaking under your breath, and so on.

Applying these principles to arguments, in the philosophical sense, will allow us to see that sometimes arguments are about what facts are relevant to the contested proposition; sometimes they are about the truth of facts admitted as relevant by all sides; sometimes both truth and relevance are in contention; and sometimes arguments are disfigured by violations of the principle of quantity. (I might just shut up, or I might filibuster.) What all this highly ramifiable field of analysis shows is that arguments are an area of contention in which conventions of goodwill can get distorted and abused. Think of the poisonous atmosphere, for example, when someone, ostensibly trying to explain his position, keeps referring to his interlocutors by abusive nicknames. Or charging them baselessly with crimes and threatening to lock them up. Or constantly responding to attempts to straighten out the argument with taunts that amount to no more than the schoolyard "I know you are, but what am I?" One of the most dismal aspects of our contemporary situation is that a powerful figure with these habits can disrupt an entire culture's capacity to reach reasonable conclusions.

We speak of arguments being lost and won. But often, really big cultural argumentative contentions are not universally recognized as lost or won. They linger and fester as unresolved arenas of disagreement, even hostility, becoming engrained and entrenched, generating their own implacable oppositions, with one side regarding as proven what the other persists in denying and vice versa. No one who has paid attention to the public life of the country over the last twenty years could doubt that this describes our situation.

The journalist David Roberts faces this in an article published by *VOX* on November 2, 2017. In "America Is Facing an Epistemic Crisis" Roberts writes of our contemporary political disagreements:

> There is no longer any settling such arguments. The only way to settle any argument is for both sides to be committed, at least to some degree, to shared standards of evidence and accuracy, and to place a measure of shared trust in institutions meant to vouchsafe evidence and accuracy. Without that basic agreement, without common arbiters, there can be no end to dispute.
>
> If one side rejects the epistemic authority of society's core institutions and practices, there's just nothing left to be done. Truth cannot speak for itself, like the voice of God from above. It can only speak through human institutions and practices.
>
> . . . What if facts and persuasion just don't matter anymore?
>
> . . . And if that's true, if the very preconditions of science and journalism as commonly understood have been eroded, then all that's left is a raw contest of power.

There is contemporary research showing that people who are presented with a reasoned appeal from the other side typically become more, not less fervent in their original opposition. As early as 2008, researchers at Dartmouth found that people receiving "corrective information" concerning their views "are likely to resist or reject arguments and evidence contradicting their opinions."[7] Wittgenstein mused in *On Certainty,* "Is it inconceivable that I should stay in the saddle, no matter how much the facts bucked?" (*OC* §616).

This effect is piled on top of simple confirmation bias, our tendency to more readily credit evidence that confirms our already established beliefs, and that piles on top of the echo-chamber effect, our tendency to seek out and attend to opinions that will buttress the ones we already have. So there are three layers here: first, we seek out differentially confirming opinions; second, we lend them more credence; and third, when confronted with counterevidence, we tend to reject it. As a result our opinion is all the stronger, having overcome challenge. It is easy to imagine the benefits of group cohesion that these tendencies could contribute to. It is also easy to cite examples from everyday political and social life where their impact causes serious, perhaps insoluble, problems.

One ploy of argumentation that will bear examining is the situation in which one party grants the other's facts as perfectly true but dismisses them with the claim "That's irrelevant!" Or even admits them as relevant but insists that they are trumped—so to speak—by other facts which are more relevant, or stronger, of greater probative force. This sort of disagreement is a disagreement about values. We tend to speak of values as if they were medium-sized pieces of dry goods. They can be held, clung to, lost, abandoned, shared, even kicked around, like metaphysical footballs. But this family of metaphors, for all its vividness, is misleading. Values aren't things of any kind, especially not metaphysical, intangible things. Values are rules of relevance. Values are the connections between things that govern what it makes sense to bring up. Values are the responses and reactions we have that incline us to say, "This case is like that one." Or "This case is not like this other one."

This means that if there is to be hope for reasonable solutions to societal oppositions, it must lie in a different kind of encounter with reasons than that offered by argument. Deliberation is different from argument in a fundamental way. The word "deliberation" comes from a Latin word meaning scales. When we deliberate, we *weigh* putative reasons. To deliberate is not to *offer* reasons but to ask of reasons that might be offered whether they are true, whether they are relevant, and—if they are true and relevant—how strong they are. Of course, two parties might differ on the questions of which putative facts are true and which are false. Two parties who are in agreement on all the facts could differ as to which facts are relevant. And parties in agreement on the truth of the facts and their relevance could differ as to which facts, pointing in different directions, are stronger. Things could fall apart at any stage and, perhaps, usually do.

But Wittgenstein's ruminations offer a way we could, possibly, keep going. Let us recall his remark about aesthetics—that its question is not "'Do you like this?' but 'Why do you like it?'"[8] The relevance of this remark grows more obvious as we move from "What is true?" to "What is relevant?" to "What is stronger?" But as Thomas Kuhn has shown in *The Structure of Scientific Revolutions,* questions about the *truth* of scientific paradigms are ultimately decided not by the weight of reasons but by something like aesthetic preferences. Scientific agreements on such large-scale paradigms as Copernican rather than Ptolemaic cosmology, relativity rather than Newtonian physics, or evolutionary theory rather than creationism, are founded on such considerations as simplicity, elegance, explanatory capacity, and coherence both internally and with other fields. All these considerations are, of course, matters of judgment. And they determine what is to count as fact and what as falsehood, whether the sun orbits the earth or vice versa, whether the movements of bodies are to be explained according to things' teleological affinity for their natural positions or the effects of gravity or the shaping of the space-time continuum and whether the diversity of living things is the result of natural selection or the direct, immediate design of an intelligent creator.

The presupposition of any argument is that each side thinks it's right and its reasons are the correct and sufficient ones. The other side, they think, has got the facts wrong or has taken the wrong facts as relevant or has weighted them inappropriately. Recognizing this range of possibilities opens a new dimension to the disagreement. Why do they accept those facts as true? Why do they think they're relevant? Why do they take them as strong enough to settle the question? At this point a part of the disagreement expands from trying to get the other side to see things as I do to trying to see how they could see them as they do. In a tough case of disagreement, we have an obligation to try to see how the other side sees the world—that is, an obligation to indwell that sensibility. That is, I have that obligation unless I am willing to fight.

Moreover, we have an obligation to examine our own senses of truth, relevance, and strength, to look critically at how and why we take things as we do, at how our natural reactions have been shaped by training and prior experience. We have to move our reactions and responses to a conscious level where we can make them the objects of critical inquiry. Two dicta of Socrates appear here. One is "The unexamined life is not worth living"; that is, unless we can bring ourselves to examine the substrata of our rationality, we are less than human. And the other: "Know thyself." When you are deliberating about questions like Wittgenstein's "Why do I like this?" what you are working on is the structure of your self. Deliberative inquiry reaches deep into the structures of our sensibilities.

How deeply it can reach is suggested by Alice Crary, who emphasized that morality (or ethics—she doesn't distinguish) is not confined to a realm of judgments with a specific moral content or quality but "involves concern for nothing less than individuals' entire personalities, the whole complicated weave of their lives."[9] And this weave is connected with the very learning of language and involves the acquisition of values: "[It] cannot help but encode a view of what matters most in life or of how best to live" (*BMJ* 43). In this she resembles Iris Murdoch, whom she quotes: a moral concept is less like a ring around a part of the world "and more like a total difference of Gestalt. We differ . . . because we see different worlds" (*BMJ* 35). And seeing different worlds is a function of the sensitivities, partially innate and partially cultivated, with which we attend to certain dimensions of the world and not others. We have no idea "what it would be for the regularities constitutive of a concept's projection to be open to view independently of sensitivities we acquire in mastering the concept" (*BMJ* 24). This means we have to give up a notion of ourselves as possessing the ability to talk about the world in a way independent of our sensitivities, and coordinately, giving up the idea of a determinate world "accessible to us independently of such sensitivities or . . . responses" (*BMJ* 26).

The liberal arts, taken as a whole, could be said to comprise those disciplines that reflect, systematically, on the emergence of meaning. Let me repeat the phrase: disciplined reflection on the emergence of meaning. It is important not to miss the complexity of structure in this formula, for it signals something that will run through all our thought about the liberal arts. The emergence of meaning suggests that something that matters is bubbling up in human experience. At this point we are not doing liberal arts yet. We are simply being human and responding to things humans are wired to respond to. "I like that." "That makes me sad." Or joyful, or angry. It is when we ask, "Why did that make me sad?" "Why do I like that?" that we enter into reflective exploration that is the liberal arts.

When Wittgenstein invoked judgment as the criterion of truth, it was not the judgment of an individual, or any individual, but social, interpersonal agreement in judgment, and not primitively, agreement on a proposition, a cognition, but agreement about how to do something—like reading a ruler or operating an electron microscope. Such agreement in judgments extend beyond doing something and include how to perceive and understand something. In giving reasons in aesthetics, I will supply facts in the attempt to get you to see things as I do. Not many years ago, many physicians believed that infants do not feel pain as older children and adults do and that their crying and avoidance of the painful stimuli were mere epiphenomena of neural discharges, unaccompanied by real pain. For that reason, and also because they were dangerous for babies, anesthetics were not used in infant surgeries. But it is unavoidable that the behaviors of infants in pain are very much like, if not identical with, behaviors we respond to as pain behaviors in children, adults, and even in animals. We cry out, grab the hurting part, whimper, and so forth. Eventually, as we learn to speak, these behaviors modulate into expressions like "Ouch!" "Ow!" and similar expressions, still accompanied by crying and the like. These behaviors are not *evidence* of pain, not outward signs of something invisible to us. They are part of pain, and recognizing them is a natural reaction, precognitively, to someone's being in pain. So powerful are these reactions that we have to be taught to ignore them when they are thought to be—as it were—false alarms. And in the consideration whether infants feel pain, sometimes it is enough to point and say: "Look at that!"

DELIBERATION: OBJECTIVITY AND CONVENTION

This point leads to another key aspect of deliberation: the necessity of objectivity. So let me address the impact of a Wittgensteinian perspective on objectivity. And at the same time, on relativism. The first lesson in my first German grammar was on relativism. Here is a part of Aufgabe Eins of *Der Anfang:* "In Amerika lernen Amerikaner Deutsch. Sie vergleichen Deutschland und Amerika und finden Deutschland klein und Amerika gross. . . . In Oesterreich finden die Oestrreicher Deutschland gross und Oesterreich klein. Alles ist relativ."[10] What that says, in essence, is that compared to America, Germany is a small country, but compared to Austria, it's a big country. Everything's relative. Austria itself is gigantic compared to Liechtenstein, an independent German-speaking country whose border it shares with Switzerland. Aha, you say. Liechtenstein—or some tiny place, somewhere—must be the absolutely smallest country. Yes, and that's a comparison, made relative to all the other countries. Every claim is made relative to some system of cognition and value. Thus the ubiquity of relativism.

In a similar way, every appeal to "be objective" must be an appeal to overcome some specific bias. Suppose you challenge me to name the greatest Green Bay Packer of the glory days in the 1960s. Plausible names might be Bart Starr, Paul Hornung, Jim Taylor, Ray Nitschke. But suppose I insist that the right answer is Elijah Pitts. "Wait a minute," you say. Because you know that I lived for twenty-four years in the small town where Pitts went to high school, and so I could plausibly have a bias in his favor. "Come on, be objective," you say. Every appeal to someone to be objective is an appeal to disregard some specific bias, and every claim to *be* objective is an implicit claim to have overcome some specifiable bias. Is there, then, no absolute objectivity, freed of every conceivable bias? That's like asking for the language that names all the colors there really are, separating every distinct hue from the next one. When we urge someone to be objective, we have to have some specific failure in mind. This is analogous to Wittgenstein's insistence throughout *On Certainty* that doubt needs a reason. If I want to raise a question, I have to employ some language I understand to do that.

Lewis Carroll's memorable poem "The Hunting of the Snark" concerns in part a map, supplied by the Bellman, that has achieved a perfection of objectivity. Let me quote three stanzas:

> He had brought a large map representing the sea,
> Without the least versatile of land:
> And the crew were much pleased when they found it to be
> A map they could all understand.
>
> "What's the good of Mercator's North Poles and Equators,
> Tropics, Zones, and Meridian Lines?"
> So the Bellman would cry, and the crew would reply,
> "They are merely conventional signs!"
>
> "Other maps are such shapes, with their islands and capes!
> But we've got our brave Captain to thank"
> (So the crew would protest) "that he's brought *us* the best–
> A perfect and absolute blank!"

The point, of course, is that without some system of largely conventional signs and symbols, established in relation each to the others—that is, relatively—we can say nothing at all about anything.

Deliberation requires us to adopt a complex posture toward our own reasons and those of others with whom we disagree. In my own case I have to regard my own reasons as open to doubt, without suspending my commitment to them; in the case of others' reasons, I have to regard them as possibly true, relevant, and sufficient, without abandoning my belief that they fall short in at least one of those dimensions. This is tricky terrain, and one is tempted to say that "true deliberation" requires reciprocity and balance. That is, each side makes itself equally vulnerable to the other and extends equal generosity to the other.

I am not saying that we are naturally disposed toward achieving this posture. It is a difficult accomplishment, and a fragile one. It has no guarantee of success, and attempting it may just get you duped and cheated.

But what would it be like to attempt to cultivate skill at deliberating? A couple of decades ago, Martha Nussbaum popularized the phrase "sympathetic imagination."[11] As she develops it, sympathetic imagination consists of three elements. The first is the embrace of a loyalty to people all over the world as the primary loyalty, subordinating national or regional loyalties to it: a kind of cosmopolitanism. The second is the ability to see oneself as bound to all peoples by ties of recognition and concern. And the third is the development of "narrative imagination," the ability to indwell the perspectives of others unlike ourselves, despite our common humanity. Because she develops this third element with skill, and because it is the posture that I am holding out as the possibility for genuine deliberation, I want to explore it at some length.

Nussbaum cites Marcus Aurelius, one of the most noted of the Stoic philosophers, a Roman emperor who conducted a seemingly endless campaign along the Rhine, defending the empire against barbarians. Aurelius recommends that "we must not simply amass knowledge; we must also cultivate in ourselves a capacity for sympathetic imagination that will enable us to comprehend the motives and choices of people different from ourselves."[12]

She cites sources from Sophocles's *Philoctetes* (409 BCE) to Ralph Ellison's *Invisible Man* (1952) to show how works of literature are critical for leading us into sympathetic understanding of the experiences of others. And this capacity, she says, is a vital function of the arts, cultivating "capacities of judgment and sensitivity that can and should be expressed in the choices a citizen makes,"[13] and it works by emphasizing the shared vulnerabilities that characterize all human lives. Nussbaum's view is subtle and nuanced, but it poses a problem that must be faced.

Those who embrace a moral core of literature use language like "leads," or "conduces," or even "poses." John Gardner wrote, in *On Moral Fiction,* that true art "is not didactic, because instead of teaching by authority and force, it explores, open-mindedly, to learn what it should teach."[14] Surely, though, Melville did not intend to leave us entirely to ourselves as to what to think of Ahab and Starbuck, of Ishmael and Queequeg. There is tension, both in the intentions of authors and in the uptake of readers, between telling and showing, between being told and catching on. And this difference corresponds to the difference between possession of an item of information, say, "Ahab is a madman," and having your sensibilities shaped by a fascinated, morally tinged, revulsion that combines with elements of attraction. The former is passively accepted; the latter is an activity. The former is an inert datum; the latter is an element in one's personal makeup.

Heraclitus, famous for emphasizing change, also said that strife is the nature of all things. Strife, or the contention between conflicting views, characterizes liberal arts. Liberal arts is not possession of a settled opinion but the constant conflict between contenders. It is an activity, not a possession. If genuine deliberation requires a context of mutual vulnerability and generosity, it needs a special context, a context protected from our reflexes of suspicion, self-interest, defensiveness, and favoritism.

This perspective explains what is meant when we say that liberal arts education is transformative. I well remember the day I was walking across the campus of Hendrix College when a student came running up to me shouting, "I've got it! I've got it." What she had got was a pretty good sense of what Kierkegaard meant by despair. She had, after wrestling with the texts, come to an understanding of that way of seeing oneself and the universe so laboriously treated in, for example, *Fear and Trembling* and *The Sickness unto Death*. And she was, perhaps a little, perhaps a lot, maybe for a while and maybe permanently, transformed. I'm not saying she was experiencing despair—there would be little to celebrate in that. Rather, she had insight into the family of sensibilities Kierkegaard wished to describe. Experiences like that one, piled up over and over again, make a liberal arts education. And they prepare one to continue having such transformative experiences.

And that is what is meant by saying that it is a process that is never completed. Part of my job at Hendrix was to give talks to prospective students and to those who had accompanied them to campus. One of the points I was eager to make was my hope that if they did come to Hendrix, they would be dissatisfied with their education. I didn't mean that the college would let them down. I meant that I hoped their liberal arts experience would open them to limitless possibilities of learning and understanding rather than giving them an education which was "completed" and "over with." Another of the great Stoics, Epictetus, this time a slave, not an emperor, stated it like this: "Sheep do not hastily throw up the grass, to show the shepherds how much they have eaten, but inwardly digesting it, they outwardly produce wool and milk."[15]

Deliberation, in demanding of us that we indwell and to the degree possible appreciate the shape and force of the other's sensibilities, requires curiosity. We have to be motivated to try to see and feel the world as the other does. That raises the question, How is curiosity stimulated? Can uncurious people become curious? Is there *instruction* in curiosity, or is it simply a dimension of one's makeup that is either present or absent?

Deliberation, in demanding of us that we indwell and to the degree possible, appreciate the shape and force of the other's sensibilities, requires imagination. We have to be able to imagine ourselves another race, another gender, another nationality, another political party, simply "other." And that raises the question, How is imagination awakened? How is it cultivated? How is it restrained and balanced by a grip on things as they are, and not set loose, like Don Quixote's imagination?

TEACHING DELIBERATION

How can we define the liberally educated person? It cannot be done according to what he or she knows, since there is no way to identify either necessary or sufficient knowledge. A liberally educated person is defined according to what she or he can do, namely, engage in deliberation. And by the possession of a disposition to deliberate. Still, knowing things is very important; if you don't know anything, you can't engage in deliberation. A liberally educated person knows how to push deliberative inquiry to consensus, or at least to clarity about being "stuck" in disagreement, and clarity about why consensus is not being reached. The liberally educated person can cope with different ways of being "stuck" and can explore them. For example, is there disagreement about the facts or about the framing or weighting of facts that are agreed upon?

If a liberally educated person is defined by characteristic skills and capacities, rather than some essential knowledge, it follows that no particular course of study designed to impart knowledge can be necessary or sufficient to impart liberal education. A student may absorb reams of information and make no progress toward becoming liberally educated, and some forms of instruction almost certainly inhibit the acquisition of liberal education. The Phi Beta Kappa Society was founded, for example, to be a discussion and debate group—a deliberative body—in frustration over the lack of opportunity for acquiring those skills through the formal curriculum of William and Mary in the late eighteenth century.

The question whether deliberation can be taught is complex, because deliberation presupposes the confluence of several epistemological states and social skills. Aristotle reminds us, early in the *Nicomachean Ethics,* that people of judgment expect a degree of precision appropriate to the subject matter. No one, he notes, tolerates probable arguments in mathematics, or expects strict demonstration from an orator. And in Plato's *Republic* we find the admonition that those who attempt to teach deliberation should avoid imparting a love of contention for its own sake, lest their students become like puppies, pulling and tearing at everything, and that it presupposes a certain level of maturity and good will.[16] From Wittgenstein we have the image of inquiry that continually passes the same landmarks, viewing the landmarks from different points of view, and gaining a sense of the terrain.

Among the constituent elements of deliberative abilities are curiosity, at least some knowledge, honesty, imagination, generosity, vulnerability, restraint, tolerance of vagueness, ambiguity, uncertainty, reciprocity, frankness, civility, and freedom of expression. In what follows, these states and skills will be arrayed to display the context in which, alone, deliberation can be practiced. We will begin, fittingly, with curiosity.

What is curiosity? The concept is, itself, a curious one. Derived from a Latin word that means "care," as a noun it can refer to something that is odd or unusual, as in "His study was filled with curiosities collected in his travels," or to a state of more or less intense interest a person might hold toward something or someone, as in "Her curiosity was boundless." It is the latter sense with which we are concerned. We can be curious about many things: an object's nature, its origins, its possible usefulness, its owner, and on and on.

Curiosity motivates many actions, from wandering on a beach to see what can be found to turning over stones looking for insects to flights to the moon. Our curiosity can be awakened by many human actions, from seeing a stranger walking down our street to hearing the distant siren of a fire engine. Natural events, too, can arouse it: How do tornadoes form? Why are summer clouds flat on the bottom?

Science—and indeed, knowledge and creativity more broadly—begin in curiosity. The story is perhaps apocryphal, but very telling, nonetheless, of Isaac Newton's curiosity being set in motion by noticing an apple's fall from its tree. That curiosity led to the law of gravity and the intellectual achievements of Newtonian mechanics. It seems that curiosity is essential to the growth of knowledge.

So what starts curiosity itself? Is it innate? Children seem naturally curious. Infants explore the world by putting things in their mouths, and older children take things apart "to see how they work." Can curiosity be taught and learned? Do people have a constant store of curiosity, or does it wax and wane? Manic states are characterized by extreme curiosity and depression by lack of interest or curiosity.

The point is not to satisfy curiosity but to keep it alive. Question leads on to question. It is an activity, not a striving for stasis. Teaching curiosity is not about giving instructions or supplying answers but about asking the right questions. According to legend, the tutors at St. John's College in Annapolis begin their seminars with a question about the text under discussion, and asking the right question to stimulate the students' curiosity is a highly valued skill, one prized by tutors and students alike.

Is curiosity ever inappropriate? What's the difference between curiosity and inquisitiveness/meddlesomeness? The phrase "curiosity killed the cat" is used in the attempt to suppress curiosity and may be a warning not to pry on pain of suffering unpleasant consequences. "None of your business!" is another attempt to suppress curiosity toward some specific topic, offering an assertion of privacy in justification.

The curiosity required by deliberation is different from the prurience exhibited by onlookers at an accident and different from the curiosity exhibited by readers of, for example, *Murder on the Orient Express*. Different still is the curiosity of the politically interested, waiting to see how an election will turn out. There are certainly more varieties, to be sure. Deliberative curiosity is the drive for conceptual understanding.

Socrates is the model of deliberative curiosity, exhibiting in the dialogues of Plato the relentless questioning that drives it. The questions resolve into two. Of every answer we can ask first, "What does that mean?" and having established that, we ask, "What reason is there to believe that it's true?" In the hands of Socrates these questions seemed endlessly recursive; that is, they can be applied to every answer, ad infinitum. Plato attempted to put an end to the recursiveness with his teaching about the Forms—abstract, intelligible concepts accessible to the mind but only imperfectly reflected in sensory objects. He held that "participation" in a Form made things what they are, from the roundness of a ball (participating in sphericity) to the justice of a particular sound judgment (participating in justice). As has been argued elsewhere in this book, there are insurmountable problems with this view, and it cannot be relied on to set determinate ends to deliberation. Deliberation comes to its end, if it does, when the parties involved agree upon a resolution.

It would be easy to neglect the important point that curiosity depends on knowledge. When we are curious, we are curious *about* something, something we already know *something* about. It makes sense to be curious about what's in a box only if we recognize it as a box that might contain something and don't, for example, take it for a solid block of wood. I can be curious as to the significance of a gesture or an unusual tone of voice only if I recognize the gesture as a gesture and detect the tone of voice as unusual.

The question, "What or how much do you need to know, before deliberation is possible?" has no general answer. Much philosophical ink has been spilled trying to define "all things considered" in the phrase "an all things considered judgment." This quickly becomes a question of relevance, which as we have noted, is itself in some sense a matter of judgment, and in another sense a matter of learning how to do something. This is what Wittgenstein meant when he wrote, "Human beings . . . agree in the language that they use. That is agreement *not in opinions but in form of life*" (*PI* §241; emphasis added).

When people attempting to deliberate disagree about what they need to agree upon before they can begin, they need to establish points of linguistic continuity—that is, meaning the same things by their words. Such exchanges as "When I say 'lie' I mean saying something you know (or have reason to believe) is false," followed by uptake that accepts my definition, or uptake that proposes modifications, would suffice. And lead on to shared knowledge.

All this so far presupposes that the interlocutors are sincere. That is, it presupposes that the parties are being honest, that they are not dissembling, not disguising their intentions or lying about what they're up to. Deliberations earnestly present themselves as being worthy of being believed, of being genuinely engaged with the other in the way in which you present yourself. In these ways deliberation is an intersubjective enterprise,[17] a "social act of mind," in the sense outlined by Thomas Reid.[18]

Imagination is the capacity to conceive, entertain, manipulate in thought, and respond emotionally to events, situations, and states of affairs that differ from reality or that may or may not come to pass in the future. When we imagine, we say, as if in the subjunctive, "What would it be like if I were . . ." or in the future tense, "What would it be like if I do . . ." The value of imagination is that through it we are able to consider counterfactuals and to lessen the grip on our understanding of the accidents of our makeup.

Over the last few years, now at an accelerating pace, American society has been struggling to dissociate itself from the emblems of the Confederacy. The Confederate flag has at last been removed from the state capitol grounds in South Carolina and from the Mississippi state flag. Statues and memorials have been removed or relocated in Charlottesville, New Orleans, Chapel Hill, and other cities. Imagination is required to grasp the differing attitudes and emotions about these actions: not only the ability but also the willingness to imagine yourself Black or white or Asian or Hispanic or of mixed race or ethnicity. When I taught at a small college in the South, a colleague kept a photograph of Robert E. Lee prominently displayed behind his desk. When the first Black member of the faculty was installed in the adjacent office, I suddenly saw that picture of Lee in a different light, as if through her eyes. Later, I learned to appreciate that it was not mere disapproval but anger that motivated someone close to me to rip Confederate flag tags off his schoolmates' pickup trucks, and I saw that it was anger rooted in sharing the feelings of his Black friends.

As noted elsewhere in this book, Martha Nussbaum in *Cultivating Humanity* emphasized the importance of narrative imagination in enabling us to conceive ourselves as occupying the standpoints of people who differ from us in race, economic status, gender, sexual orientation, nationality, ethnicity, profession, health, or stage of life. While part of the point of being able to do these things is to enable us to view the world more nearly as others do, and significant benefit lies in acquiring the ability to view our own perspective, as it were, from the outside. It was Robert Burns who summed this up succinctly, in his "To a Louse":

> O wad some Power the giftie gie us
> To see oursels as ithers see us
> It wad frae mony a blunder free us
> An' foolish notion
> What airs in dress an' gait wad leave us
> An' ev'n devotion!

Willingness to consider the possibility of alternative perspectives can even loosen our most deeply held "devotions."

And this, of course, requires courage. It requires courage because genuine deliberation places our most deeply held beliefs and values in play, making them vulnerable to assessment, critique, and possible amendment or even rejection. To be able to face such a prospect requires, in turn, a social setting of immense restraint, an awareness of the vulnerability not only of ourselves but also of our interlocutors. How far this is from the aggressive and defensive style that characterizes debate! It also involves generosity, the willingness to explore the other's avowals for a sense in which they are most plausible, not taking things at their least plausible. There must also be tolerance of vagueness, ambiguity, and uncertainty, while the parties deliberating probe for common ground.

The additional skills and capacities needed for deliberation listed above—reciprocity, frankness, civility, and freedom of expression—are included in their most straightforward and obvious meanings and require no further explication.

A cardinal point in closing: no single standard of mixing and balancing these skills can be formulated in advance to govern a deliberative process. There will be multiple models, and the judgments about just which skills to call into service, at just what point, is itself a part of the deliberative skill set.

4

WHAT IS THE LIBERAL ARTS CANON AND HOW IS IT JUSTIFIED?

FIRST, LET ME OFFER a brief recapitulation of the argument so far. In chapter 2, I presented the case for believing that the best account we can give of a proposition's being true is that it is what people will reliably agree on. This is because we lack access to an unmediated reality. Everything we know and do is shaped by the sensitivities of our organs of perception, filtered by the concepts of our language, and formed by the actual practices our communities of action and discourse. This means, as Wittgenstein observed, that human agreement determines what is true or false. Not one person's determination but the agreement of those who have been trained into competent operation with the concepts involved. Remember the remark that "agreement" and "rule" are cousins. Teaching one involves teaching the other. And training, in order to succeed, relies on uptake, an unlearned responsiveness that enables the trainee to "get it." Which means that at the bottom of a chain of reasons there will be something that is not a reason. Explanations come to an end. So the deepest layers of our attempts to understand our arguments finally reach something like aesthetic considerations.

Then in chapter 3 I started from a different standpoint and asked the value of education in the liberal arts, reviewing the commonly met-with accounts. I described Phi Beta Kappa's inquiry into that question and our discovery that the beneficiaries of liberal arts typically told us that the acquisition of skills of deliberation and of the disposition to deliberate were the most valuable lasting aspects of their education. I then distinguished deliberation from argument, using as a tool Wittgenstein's remark that "the question of Aesthetics was not 'Do you like this?' but '*Why* do you like it?'"[1] The question *why* we like something penetrates to our capacities for feeling and understanding, the training we've received, and ultimately to unlearned patterns of uptake and response that are the product of our evolutionary history. To deliberate is to reflect on the way that those patterns serve as sources for the reasons we give both in our own case and in the cases of others with whom we are deliberating. We argue by trying to get the other person to "see things" as we do, to "take" things in the way that we "take" them. And we deliberate by attempting to understand and assess *why* we see things as we do, and *why* our interlocutor sees things differently.

THE PROBLEM OF CANON

Now I want to circle round to yet another point—as it were—on the periphery of our topic, and go into it from yet another angle, an angle that will show us many of the same landmarks from yet another perspective. Aristotle's *Nicomachean Ethics* will be our point of departure, opening, as it does, with the remark that every human activity aims at some end. In the spirit of that remark, we can ask, "At what end does liberal education aim?" The obvious and seemingly uninformative answer is that liberal education aims at the production of the liberally educated person. But we know what that is, if we are to believe those members of Phi Beta Kappa who participated in our exercise: a liberally educated person is a person who can deliberate well and who is inclined to do so. We now have the questions that will guide this chapter: How can people best be taught to deliberate well, and how can they best become *inclined* to deliberate well? Notice that the first question is about imparting skills and capacities, while the second is something like aesthetic or affective. It's about shaping people's tendencies to behave in certain ways. That raises further questions about authority, which we will have to explore.

I will begin by setting out three aspects of the apparent answer to these questions and then proceed to show that those aspects are false or seriously misleading. First, it seems, for reasons I will provide, that there must be a more or less fixed canon of great texts constituting the core reading list of persons who are to be trained to deliberate. Second, it seems necessary for there to be a standard and prescribed mode of appropriating those texts, a standard way of receiving the values embodied in them, and conveyed through them, such that failure to derive *this* set of values from those texts constitutes *mis*understanding. Third, it seems necessary that there should be a set of abstract principles, expressing the core values that are expressed through those texts, illustrated through instantiation in concrete examples. Why do these three things—the texts, the mode of their appropriation, and the principles expressed in them—need to be fixed in advance, in effect, in order for training in deliberation to occur?

Aristotle, early in the *Nicomachean Ethics,* makes an interesting remark about the study of ethics: "To be a competent student of what is right and just, . . . one must first have received a proper upbringing in moral conduct. The acceptance of a fact as a fact is a starting point. . . . A man with this sort of background has or can easily acquire the foundations from which he must start." Aristotle seems to say that only those who have been well brought up can even understand the points at issue in discussions of what is right and wrong, that until we have been trained into some community of practical ethics—trained to follow rules and by following them learned what is and what is not following them—we cannot enter into their critical examination. And that seems right. So if our moral education is to be broader than the narrow span of our own experience—if it is to profit from the experiences of others, historical and fictitious, and if it is to initiate us into a community of shared values, there must be a fixed and circumscribed set of texts (or stories, if we are a preliterate society) supplying the examples of excellence, fit behavior, corruption, dishonor, etc., on which we are to learn to agree.

Moreover, if we are to learn to agree about such things, we will have to be taught to agree about them—instructed to recognize good and evil, virtue and wickedness. That is, we will have to be instructed, or rather trained, in the proper uptake of exemplars of good and bad. Remember Wittgenstein's remark that the concept "agreement" and the concept "rule" are cousins, that we learn them together. And in order to be able to generalize, we will have to abstract the essence from the cases we have learned to agree about and successfully identify it elsewhere, in new cases.

To move from one case to the next and recognize it as similar and apply the concept is the sense of "only connect," the epigraph of E. M. Forster's *Howard's End.* So there are the three elements: sources of exemplars (texts, as I am using for shorthand), training in recognizing their meaning, and abstraction of fixed essences. Without these, moral training looks impossible, and deliberation is a nonstarter.

Yet there are good reasons to be leery of each of these elements of fixity. The idea of a canon of fixed texts is coordinate with the idea of a community that is committed to that canon, so in order to make sense of the one, we must examine the other. What is a community? This is an exceedingly complicated question, but its root surely is the notion of a group identity. But what grouping identifies a woman in her thirties who is Caucasian, American, a southerner, a Methodist, a mother, a divorcee, a PEO, and a Rotarian, among other groupings that could be mentioned? We have to acknowledge that communities are overlapping and not mutually exclusive, that they bear with different degrees of seriousness, or weight, on determining who or what a person "really" is, and that to insist on some one grouping of texts as definitive is a kind of essentialism, a stipulation, which would require justification.

Conversely, if it is unclear what community membership defines an individual, it is equally unclear what individuals compose a community. How frequent a patron do you have to be to be a "regular" at a bar? Is "regular" church attendance three times a week or three times a month? While many communities, for example, the US Marine Corps, are sharply bounded—that is to say, you're either in or you're out and it's clear which—many communities are vaguely bounded, like Steelers fans or Red Sox fans. And that vagueness extends to their attachment to the exploits of their exemplars—like Franco Harris's Immaculate Reception or Big Papi's home runs at Fenway.

Moreover, communities change. There are schisms, secessions, unifications, etc. And even without changes of that sort, communities are typically sustained by evolving conceptions of the goods for the sake of which they exist. Alasdair MacIntyre, who developed this notion extensively in his *After Virtue*, argued that continuing conflict over a culture's central aims and values is a characteristic feature of any living tradition.[2] And to the extent that such conflict is continuous, it will involve conflict regarding the sources of the exemplars to be looked to as providing the classic cases from which principles are derived: there can be no absolute fixity among the texts.

Let's take up the problem about the meaning of exemplars, the cases of right and fit behavior, wickedness and corruption, that are the groundwork of our concepts of good and evil. Even if we agree on the critical texts, it could be argued that we need definitive guidance on uptake. What is to keep us from admiring the wrong people and condemning the virtuous? Here is the relevant concern:

> If the point of providing the novices of our culture with examples of action and deliberation as the starting points of moral reflection is to provide them with examples of virtue

> and vice as examples of excellence and failure, then some provision will have to be made for enabling the novices to distinguish and recognize the cases for what they are. Either the texts themselves shall have to identify the cases of excellence *as* cases of excellence, and cases of failure *as* cases of failure. Or the novices will have to have received some type of training antecedent to and/or simultaneous with exposure which will enable them to recognize [them as such].[3]

At stake here is the idea that we cannot tell what an exemplar comes to unless someone tells us. And it also seems to be implied that if we are told, we cannot resist the instruction. (If we could resist, what good would the instruction do?) But surely the right response to this insistence on designating heroes and villains as such is that it makes the student (or "novice") the passive recipient of information in a dynamic that is critically constituted by his or her active, participatory stance toward the exemplar. You can't tell someone how to feel, how to react, how to "take" a stimulus.

Jaroslav Pelikan, former dean of the Yale Graduate School, addressed this issue in an essay called "King Lear or Uncle Tom's Cabin?"[4] Pelikan contrasts two different styles in which values may be present in literature; in *King Lear,* values are implicit in the narrative and actions of the characters; they are gathered through induction from the texture of the action; they are handled analytically, as objects of investigation and consideration. As Pelikan puts it, they are not so much "taught" as "caught." On the other hand, *Uncle Tom's Cabin* presents values that are explicit, deductive, in that they are virtually necessitated by the action, and didactic—given to the reader unmistakably, as information. But, again, the point is that the action should awaken responses in the reader, not merely convey data. The deductive, didactic approach attempts both too much and too little: too much control and too little opportunity for transformation.

The attempt to close and fix the meanings of exemplars also forfeits one of the great pleasures, and one of the most instructive aspects of reading—or, properly, of rereading. I first became acquainted with Sophocles's great tragedy *Antigone* in the late 1960s. It was the age of Vietnam and of the civil rights movement. It was clear to me, then, that Antigone, the character, insisting on observing her religious duty toward her brother's body, slain in revolt against Thebes, embodied the righteousness of the individual moral conscience, and that Creon, her father, the king of Thebes, in forbidding her the performance of those duties and executing her for performing them, was a Nixonian villain, bent on preserving his own hold on power, even at the price of corrupting his own religious duties. All was quite clear.

The next time I turned seriously to study *Antigone,* I had been a dean for a half dozen years. My, how those characters had changed. Instead of a self-sacrificing hero, the character Antigone resembled one of those monomaniacal faculty members for whom defeat was the sweetest victory, who would find a way to lose and waste everyone's time in faculty committees doing so. And Creon seemed then be the man of virtue with the distasteful job of managing a situation in which the opposing sides are both right and both wrong. It was again all quite clear, but different.

This example seems instructive because we do respond in ways that reflect our own experiences, and different experiences give us different uptakes. I could cite a number of similar examples from my own experience, including my increasing identification with Pierre on successive readings of *War and Peace*.

Finally, let me take up the matter of the relation between exemplars and the principles they represent. Again I will remind you of Wittgenstein's remark about the concept "rule" and the concept "agreement." We can have rules because we can agree in judgments. And judgments are about cases—that is, about exemplars. We learn rules by learning how to judge. A principle is a rule abstracted from our acquaintance with cases. It is in cases that principles are rooted; the cases have priority. Aristotle, in the *Nicomachean Ethics,* comes down to a definition of excellence that he famously defines as a mean, identified by reason, relative to oneself, and identified, furthermore, "as a person of practical wisdom" would do. This is the big point again: we cannot understand principles unless we are familiar with cases. And the chief utility of liberal arts education is to impart familiarity with cases and to jump-start the deliberative life by its practice.

The liberal arts curriculum must provide exemplars. There are various senses in which that happens, various ways in which the student is acculturated into different communities. One of the things a chemist does in teaching chemistry is to exemplify how chemists think, to show by doing how they define problems and seek to solve them. These processes take place with differing intensity and depth, depending on whether the student is in a general education chemistry course, perhaps their only one, or in an advanced major's course or conducting research under faculty supervision. Learning to become a chemist is more than memorizing the periodic chart; it involves coming to indwell the world seen as structured by those elements and their interaction.

HOW IS CANON ESTABLISHED?

So how do we approach the question of canon? Again the answer can be approached through Heraclitus's concept of strife. The question of canon exists in a field of tension between two poles. One pole is the idea of a fixed canon, supplying fixed exemplars, illustrating settled intellectual and moral conclusions. This pole is deadening and dead. The other pole is the denial of canon as such, with such exemplars as arise in whatever texts are read utterly open to interpretation, yielding intellectual and moral chaos. This pole is lively but completely lacking in order. We will never escape the pull of both poles. Our task is to find ways that yield order without being deadly and supply room for innovation and improvement without producing chaos. One model for such a way is the deliberative conversation, in which reasons are adduced and examined, offered and challenged.

In fact, we have such a process. Its participants are those who argue for conservation or innovation, for preservation and transmission or upheaval and transformation, for uniformity or diversity. Compare the typical undergraduate core curriculum of 1950—shaped by Columbia's civilization courses, Chicago's Great Books, and the recommendations of Harvard's *Red Book*—with the current undergraduate curriculum, in all its variety and with all its contentions. How have these changes occurred?

They have occurred through the efforts of faculty committees, of individual scholars and thinkers, through the often slow processes of shaping opinion within communities that are sometimes ill-defined and worse organized. They have occurred through drift. There is something in the world of intellectual fashion analogous to genetic drift, which is based on analogy with literal drifting with the external currents, and according to which ideas and concepts wax and wane and interact with each other in ways that no one quite controls.

It is the concept, the idea that no one controls the evolution of commons and curriculum, that is most important. No one controls the process definitively; that is to say, no one can stipulate its proceedings or its outcomes. But it is possible to steer the process toward a more thoroughly deliberative character. Making the process more deliberative would be to refine it, focusing disagreements on particular moments of uptake and response, moments of difference in assessment of the relevance of particular facts, moments of difference in the weighting of facts that point in opposing directions and opportunities for approaching resolution through agreement. Above all, making the process more deliberative ensures that it does not get broken off by stipulation or some other form of coercion. We are in a process that focuses on what it is important for students to read, but at the other end of the continuum, there is the burning of books.

Let me turn now to the question of personal transformation and the assumption of authority to attempt such a thing. By what authority do we claim to offer the transformative power of liberal arts education? The difficulty is that we can't explain, not fully, anyway, the end we are aiming at and the transformation we propose to aim for, until the student is far down the road that leads there. That is what makes liberal arts education different from delivery of goods and services to a consumer, and it is this that severely limits the adequacy of an economic model for understanding the successes and failures, the efficiencies and the wastes, of liberal education. The student is not a consumer, not a customer. The point of an education is not to gratify the student's desires but to bring them to have different and better desires. The student is someone partially in our care, moving toward being a different sort of someone, someone whom we can't fully explain yet. Signing on for this journey takes trust, and that makes the authority question all the more piquant.

Maybe the problem is in the connotations of the noun "transformation." In the fairy tale the princess's kiss transforms the frog into a handsome prince. A bite of the queen's apple transforms Snow White into somnolence. A night of restless dreams transforms Gregor Samsa into a giant vermin. In each case the transition is instantaneous and passive. But what we aim for is neither achieved instantaneously nor acquired passively. Becoming liberally educated takes time, and it critically requires the active participation of the student. Waving a wand is one thing. It is altogether different to offer opportunities, incentives, means, and encouragement, seeking to engage an activity of self-development.

So what opportunities do we offer? We offer the prospect of coming to have better opinions. Here are four characteristics of better opinions. First, better opinions are connected in consistent ways with other opinions. Worse ones are isolated, at best unconnected with one's other views on things and at worst actually inconsistent with them. So one of the ways we improve our opinions is by exploring for and rooting out inconsistencies. The growth of better views on the relations of people from different ethnic backgrounds or different racial origins, or improvements in the status of women, must be due to a process operating over centuries that has brought people to see the inconsistency in treating one sort of human being differently from some other sort of human being. Surely, too, this seeking out inconsistencies lies behind Jeremy Bentham's recommendation that any being's deserving moral regard is not the answer to the question "Can it reason?" but the answer to the question "Can it suffer?"

Second, better opinions also stand in networks of supporting evidence. Different beliefs can be consistent without offering mutual support. I believe that Plato wrote the *Symposium* and that Vermeer painted the *View of Delft*. These views are consistent, but neither gives me reason for believing the other. Another kind of connection between opinions can be illustrated by the standing of evolutionary theory in modern biology. This is not just a question of evidence, but of coherence and mutual fit. Everything that is known about the mechanisms of genetics, about the distribution of similar species across the earth, about the adaptations of flu viruses, and on and on make sense only in the context of an overarching evolutionary vision of the nature of life. Better opinions are connected in patterns of mutual support and confirmation.

Third, worse opinions are barren; they lead nowhere. Like false assumptions or red herrings in mystery novels, bad opinions lead us into blind alleys, while better opinions suggest ways forward.

Fourth, worse opinions are stultifying. Like prejudices that shut us off from appreciating the fullness of another's humanity, they diminish our own humanity. Better opinions, on the other hand, lead to growth, to fuller humanity, to richer takes on things.

Worse opinions are disconnected, unsupported by reasons, lacking in suggestiveness for further understanding, and not conducive to the acquisition by their bearers of greater skills and capacities. Better opinions are coherently connected, supported by reasons, fertile with suggestions for further understanding, and conducive to the bearer's further growth. Coming to possess the skills of deliberation is a matter of learning how to gain such better opinions. It is tempting to say, at this point, that the authority we want to claim is self-evident. How could anyone not wish to replace worse opinions with better ones?

But I think this appeal to self-evidence is not a comfortable resting place. Certain as we are that we are right, it is also certain that the self-evidence of one age is the unexamined prejudice of another. We need to build in some kind of principle that would guarantee that opinions of the sort we're describing are more nearly true, like an asymptotic curve, approaching a line it can, by its very nature, never reach. But for that we'd need a standpoint that provided perspective on both curve and line. But recall that the line is by definition not accessible. This is a wish that cannot be satisfied. There can be no guarantee, and we'll have to live with that. What is important is recognizing that we have to live with discomfort. This is not the discomfort of not being able to say that we are right and the Nazis wrong but the discomfort of lacking an appeal beyond the consensus of people we respect and trust to establish it. Just as logic will not come and take you by the throat, so will morality not come and take you by the heart.

Why can't we say more clearly and finally what liberal education is? Well, what shape is a cat? What configuration in its active and ever-changing life do we want to say is the definitive one? It may turn out that defining liberal education is like that odd moment when people overhear each other talking in distant rooms and one of them yells "What?" And the others yells back, "I'm not talking to you!" Notice that in order to do its work, that claim has to be false. When I tell you I'm not talking to you, I most certainly am talking to you. And so when we say we don't know what liberal arts education is, embedding that claim in the right way in the right sort of education, we may be showing that we do know what it is. This is a high hope and connects with Socratic irony and with the skills of coping with subject matter that fades in and out, coming into and out of focus.

There are many reasons for the difficulty in giving a stable account of liberal education. But the central reason is that there is, in the nature of things, no bird's-eye view of it, no synoptic view, no stable summary. As there is no uniquely adequate map of reality but many maps, depending on what interests and capacities you bring to their construction, so the shape of liberal education, and its apparent value, will look different when viewed as job preparation, as cultural initiation, as pursuit of the intrinsically worthwhile, or from any number of other standpoints. The point is to get used to this situation, to resist without embarrassment the urge to have a final, adequate account and to learn to swim, not to stand.

Socrates hung out in the Athenian agora, asking pesky questions. There was always someone—usually a slightly oafish young man—ready to take the bait. "Oh, I know what piety is," says Euthyphro. "Oh, I can tell you what justice is," says Thrasymachus. Socrates has feigned ignorance, but it turns out he has a better notion of the subject at hand than any of the galoots who claim to be able to define it. But then it also turns out that Socrates's understanding, better as it is, and empowered as it is for improvement by being honed on the mistakes and misunderstandings all around, is not fully adequate. Even the wisest can't close the discussion with ultimate answers. The trick is to keep the conversation going in the face of reasonable prospect that it has no end.

This is familiar stuff that many of us got as first-year students. The really important questions elude final answers. And yet skeptical indifference is not a real-life option. This is the built-in tension in any responsible approach to the big questions and part of our acculturation as educated persons. Part of our becoming grown-up about big questions was learning to accept this fact cognitively and then learning to adjust to it existentially. It requires adaptation to Heraclitus's principles, not only that everything changes, but the deeper point that such stability as there is, like the changes, is the product of tension between opposing forces.

So why, then, do we forget it when we set out to explain the very most important part of what we do when we talk about liberal education? Why do we take ourselves to task for failing at something we shouldn't expect, namely, to give an account of liberal education that will lie still while we attempt its vivisection? If you want something to lie still for the anatomist, you'd better kill it first. On the other hand, if you want to understand how the living thing operates, you had better expect it to dance out of the frame, to look different from different angles, and to have multiple processes having complementary but different purposes. Living processes do things as different as eating, breathing, reproducing, sleeping, and casting off waste. What, again, *is* the shape of a cat?

It's easy to see why we are in this predicament. Two forces converge to drive it from our minds. The first is our need to justify liberal education to a public that may or may not have any idea what it is and that may or may not have any sympathy for its values. We fear that it is in constant danger of being left behind in the march of academic pursuits that are specialized, technical, vocational, or professional—in a word, obviously useful. This threat is very real, and perennial. Liberal arts education will require being reexplained and redefended in every age. The narrower your view of what counts, the more confined your scope of interest, the sharper your case for and against will be, and the more you can discount as not mattering. Conversely, the broader your scope, the more diffuse your focus, and the more you will seem to need to be taking everything into account all at once. Critics always take the strategy of narrowing the focus for a sharper cut.

This leads to the second force: the urge to conform to our cultural penchant for the sharp, concise statement. We think we need to say something simple and convincing, something that conveys certainty. When you blend the defensiveness with the need for concision and certainty, you brew the elixir that makes us forget what we know: it isn't simple and it isn't certain—at least, no formulations are simple and certain. We need the courage to say this at the same time as we continue to advance the arguments we know so well: that knowledge and cultivation are good for their own sakes; that a comprehensive understanding of things, pressed as far as the limits of our grasp will go, is part of individual human flourishing; that the sorts of professions in which we are likely to succeed require just the sort of supple, critical, liberal, inquisitive, truth-seeking, reason-giving spirit that the liberal arts help to foster; and that the survival of democracy—in this country, let alone in the far reaches of the world—seems to depend on that same range of capacities and inclinations extended into political life. It's not simple, but it is terribly important.

I have alluded at several points to the irony of our situation. The very day I composed the sentence that closes the last paragraph, a letter fell on my desk from a Phi Beta Kappa chapter secretary, opening its second paragraph with this plea: "Also please send me your definition of 'the Liberal Arts.' Some of our members think the phrase is passé, and even think it is our duty to award our scholarships to SCIENCE MAJORS. The stated goals of Jefferson's founding of our Society need to be clarified.... Send me any data you can."

Where to begin responding? To the horror of both Aristotle and Alice, I will begin at the end. How can I explain the liberal arts by sending data? There is a rough cognitive continuum that *begins* with data and runs through information to knowledge, then to understanding, and finally fetches up at wisdom. I could have tried to comply with the request to send wisdom, not because I am wise, but because a question about wisdom is a question about the meaning of things, the patterns in things that we grasp when we understand the knowledge we have assembled from information derived from data. The data the writer requested are about four levels of cognitive sophistication away from where we need to be.

I'm being too hard on the writer. Yes, I am. But I have a point to make, or several. Jefferson played no role in founding Phi Beta Kappa, having been a student at William and Mary decades before. He was in the Flat Hat Club, an organization he said had "no useful object." And the natural sciences—physics, chemistry, biology, and so on—are squarely at the core of the liberal arts. But the real issue is the first request: "Please send me your definition of 'the Liberal Arts.'" This reminds me of the offers of the great barbecue houses in Memphis, places like the Rendezvous and Corky's, that will ship ribs anywhere on earth: vacuum wrapped and frozen solid.

But of course, to give the other perspective its due, we couldn't even articulate the interesting and interestingly endless questions unless we were first able to talk about the liberal arts as consisting in subject matter of this sort and not that, and liberal education as consisting of processes of this sort and not that. I had and have an obligation to say something helpful, as long as I don't convey the impression that liberal arts can be made to lie too still on the anatomist's bench or freeze-dried too snugly for long-distance shipping. The point is to learn to expect the right sort of thing from conversations about defining the liberal arts.

What can we expect? We can't expect the culminating discovery, the ultimate articulation, the final, best way of putting it that brings the process to fruition. That summons the image of philosophical argument envisaged decades ago by Robert Nozick in his *Philosophical Explanations*. Philosophers sometimes seem to wish, wrote Nozick, for arguments so strong that their opponents would have to accept them or die. But "No!" he says. Even that wouldn't be strong enough, since some people might choose death. What we want is an argument so strong that not even death can absolve the other person of admitting that you are right. But this wish is an authoritarian fantasy. There's always another angle, another perspective.

In Joseph Conrad's *Lord Jim,* there is a parable told by an old German sea captain named Stein about how being born into the world is like falling into the sea. "If he tries to climb out into the air as inexperienced people endeavor to do, he drowns—*nicht wahr?* . . . No, I tell you. The way is to the destructive element submit yourself, and with the exertions of your hands and feet in the water make the deep, deep sea keep you up."[5]

This resolve has been stigmatized by a blogger, in the *Chronicle,* Laurie Fendrich, under the title "I Argue, Therefore, I Am." She has put us on notice about something called "the argumentative theory of reasoning." Also known, she says, as "the social brain hypothesis," this view is being touted as the threatening new challenge to "almost all classical philosophy" and to the liberal arts' reliance on the cultivation of "critical thinking" as one of its principal justifications. Fendrich says that what is called in question is "the unexamined idea that reasoning is about individuals examining their unexamined beliefs in order to discover the truth." In place of this noble principle, what we get with the argumentative theory of reasoning is the view that argumentative thought, rooted in evolutionary development, exists to help us win arguments. It's not about truth. It's about making the better argument. I want to critique this challenge in closing as a summary of my project.

Fendrich concludes that this idea needs our attention partly because it challenges the deep rationale of critical thinking and partly because it has quite striking pedagogical consequences. It valorizes social argument, as opposed to solitary ratiocination, and the teaching method it suggests would require more confrontation with opposing thought. But because it denies that reason is a truth-seeking activity, it seems to deny the fundamental premise of rational inquiry. So she calls it a "depressing advance in the history of thought."

Fendrich references Hugo Mercier and Dan Sperber's "Why Do Humans Reason? Arguments for an Argumentative Theory." The theory looks like an advance because it comes draped in the authority of evolutionary psychology. It might be, she suggests, "the next popular movement in higher education," with all the prestige of evolutionary grounding behind it.

There is also a pedagogical consequence: if we accepted "the argumentative theory of reasoning," wouldn't we conclude that the best way to prepare people for good, reflective lives would be to assemble them in small groups for guided, argumentative, and then deliberative, discussion of important topics, believing that the views that prevail in such discussions are, over the long haul, the best we can do for truth and that the skills there acquired—including not only critical acuity but imaginative sympathy as well—will acquit people well in later life? We would call those sessions "liberal arts seminars."

But is this view a new one? No, it isn't. It's another version of a minority report that has been filed, over and over again, in the history of thought, to the effect that our inclination to conceive reason as a truth-seeking organ (Richard Rorty's phrase, I believe) is symptomatic of misplaced intellectual ambitions and that, therefore, coming to terms with what reasoning *can* legitimately do for us requires our first learning to abjure the craving to have what it can't deliver. That craving is for final and unassailable possession of truth, or, if you like, *Truth,* a possession that claims reason, or, if you like, *Reason,* as its warrant. The minority report suggests that we need to work past this lure and to come to understand reasoning as a human social process and cultivate it for the good that it can deliver.

Who has filed this report? The ancient Greek Sophists, for example: Protagoras and the other Sophists, who got such bad press in Plato. David Hume. Ludwig Wittgenstein, as we have seen, in his second philosophical mood. Friedrich Nietzsche, who combined a critique of the pretensions of reason with an unmasking of its role as a disguise for the exercise of power. And surely our recent flirtation with deconstruction had about it this deflationary account of the role and scope of reason. The idea that reasoning is not humanity's participation in the Grand Logic of Reality but is, instead, a cluster of techniques for wringing sense out of experience, is an idea that some voices in the philosophical tradition have been advancing for a long time.

And not just in the West. Nagarjuna's demolition of abstract reasoning in a Buddhist context, much in the Taoist tradition, and the confluence of such strands in Zen share in the project of working through and past the pretensions of reason to deliver absolute truth.

This minority report has been stigmatized as "skepticism," and its critics have claimed that it opens the door to nihilism, the uncritical affirmation of unquestioned traditions, the glorification of power and violence, radically unresolvable relativism, and so on. And it does open the door to them all in this sense: if you are hell-bent on arriving at one of those terrible destinations, reason will not stop you. Reason alone will not prevent the intellectual justification of moral catastrophe, no matter what your theory about it. Fendrich notes that the argumentative theory of reasoning is self-referential. Since it is itself a product of reasoning, it cannot claim to be true in any transcendent sense. It's only a view that will win the argument. Since the same would be true of any alternative, this consideration appears on both sides of every comparative equation. We have known at least since Kant that reason, left to itself, is plagued with what he called paralogisms and antinomies.

And we have Wallace Stevens to tell us, when our view strikes the palm at the end of the mind, "that it is not the reason / That makes us happy or unhappy."[6] Or good or bad, either. Though reason, or reasoning, is what we have to work with, and it is well to keep in mind some of the complexities long since discovered about how it works.

5

LIBERAL ARTS IN A GLOBAL CONTEXT

THE PROBLEM NOW TO be confronted is the nature of the liberal arts vis-à-vis popular and philosophical attitudes about truth, relativism, and objectivism.

One could be forgiven for being reminded of the story of the great New England transcendentalist Margaret Fuller, whose habitual affirmation of the grand scope and sway of things was to declaim the welcoming pronouncement, "I accept the universe!" Word of Fuller's embrace reached the cranky English intellectual Thomas Carlyle, who is reputed to have rejoined, "Gad! She'd better!" Likewise, the global nature of our present life had better make a difference in how we shape liberal education. The question is not whether we will accept globalization but whether we will accept and work productively within the myriad ways in which globalization will shape us.

Here we can think of Bertrand Russell's distinction between the sort of reality possessed by Hamlet on the one hand and that possessed by Napoleon on the other: "If no one thought about Hamlet, there would be nothing left of him; if no one had thought about Napoleon, he would have soon seen to it that someone did!"[1] If we don't move ourselves to think about our global context, the world will see to it that we do, with an impact we might not have chosen, had we taken the lead ourselves. So the project is upon us: we can shape our response to globalization or have it shaped for us. There can be no question which course to choose.

THE IRONY OF GLOBALIZATION

As we shape our response, we had better be ready for a great irony. The modern world has been formed by the rationalization of all the processes of our lives into more orderly, more productive, more efficient means/ends relationships. The big characteristic of our lives along these lines, as we have discovered over the past couple of centuries, is that we have gotten much better at betting what we know we want. For the privileged sectors of the world, and the privileged sectors of populations within all sectors, this has been a great boon.

But the results are only as good as what we knew to seek and only as easy and untroubled as the means we knew to deploy. So while we are getting better and better at getting what we knew we wanted, we are worse and worse at coping with the consequences of not having understood what we ought to have wanted. We find that we did not understand the relationship between some things that we wanted and other things we definitely did not want, and continue not to want, even though we are getting them. We do not know what to do about the goods that are left out of our means/ends calculations or how to balance competitive and incompatible ends. We do not know how to deal with unintended consequences; we have, really, no clue how to deal with the pressing need to deliberate in choosing ends and to come to terms with competing claims in choosing means. We are set up, then, for the ironic realization of all sorts of things we did not intend and perhaps could not have imagined.

Let me label this predicament the irony of globalization. Simply put, it is this: what we should have expected to be a rich feast of unparalleled diversity may well turn out, instead, to be an unmanageable, unintelligible smorgasbord in which the cultural treasures of the world are thrown before us for our delectation and reduced to trivial status by the very richness and variety of their simultaneous appearance. The world threatens to arrive, deracinated and in piecemeal fashion, like the biggest, brightest, most succulent produce section of the best market ever. And we will look on, thinking, "How interesting. How pretty. How amazing. How different." And our capacities for choice—which are, after all, what we signed up to cultivate—will be at first bewitched by just those features. The market has prepared us for this. We are trained to respond to whatever is interesting, pretty, amazing, and different. We have even been taught to shop. We will select whatever strikes our fancy, seeking to secure it, of course, at the cheapest price possible.

No less than kiwifruit, the market will bring us Maori mythology, with quite likely, no more impact on our sense of what things mean or what we should want out of life or what life wants out of us than the appearance of a strange, delicious new fruit. The global market of ideas, images, stories, ways of being in the world, is likely merely to complicate our occasions of meaningful choice with new options without offering us any compensating advantage in the process we wanted to carry forward, namely, developing, cultivating, and refining our ability to understand what things mean and thus to make good choices.

The real danger is that the mode of choosing that such markets thrust upon us will simply be reinforced. Willy-nilly, then, by bringing us the treasures of the world to delight in and contemplate, higher education will drive us further into the identity of consumers, those who simply take in, use up, and discard whatever they have recently found to be interesting, pretty, amazing, or different. All we have to do is glide along in the globalizing world, and it will happen. The universally engulfing nature of market forces will ensure that.

It was Marx and Engels who saw that the market creates a reality that drives all others out of existence. Before it, they wrote, "All that is solid melts into air."[2] Globalization turns this melting pot into a blast furnace. Unimaginably more arrives to be melted into commodities that will be worth just what the market says.

Am I saying that globalization is a bad thing? By no means. Let's look at some of the good things it brings. First, because a global perspective means a perspective that incorporates diversity, a certain characteristic distortion of the agenda of liberal education becomes more difficult to achieve. In such contexts, one doesn't say that something becomes impossible, because there is no agenda that someone, somewhere will not be moved to advance. But here's something that used to be alluring and even easy: the Whiggish interpretation (named for Herbert Butterfield's 1931 book, *The Whiggish Interpretation of History*).

This is the perspective expressed in the title of my sixth-grade world history textbook, *Prelude to American Greatness.* Even then I knew there was something fishy about that. But there it was: Look, here are the Athenians inventing democracy for us. And there are those rugged barons, standing up for us at Runnymede in 1215. We needed to read Locke because he outlined what Jefferson got clearly. The Whiggish interpretation of history is the view that the past is prologue, the propaedeutic to the pinnacle we have achieved. How nice of the Hebrews to have collected all that literature awaiting its Christian interpretation, and how considerate of Australopithecus, to blaze the evolutionary trail toward us. Whiggish interpretations are a constant temptation.

But they are harder to make plausible when we are confronted with meanings and values that simply can't be appropriated as steps on the way to us. So there is a kind of Copernican revolution here. As Copernicus displaced humanity from the center of the universe, so globalization displaces us from the center of history. It makes it harder—not, as I just mentioned, impossible—to tell an us-centered triumphalist story that gathers the whole sweep into one tale of progress.

By the same token it makes it harder to tell the same story upside down. I mean the story that finds Western civilization to be a sorry sequence of oppression, exploitation, and enslavement. There has been plenty of all those things. But the sensibility that finds all and only of the worst of humanity's crimes in the chronicles of the West becomes less plausible in the face of the comparable narratives of deplorable wickedness and shameful behavior wherever we look. The self-centeredness of finding the West uniquely culpable becomes likewise more difficult to sustain.

Pulling these claims together, we can say that globalization makes it more difficult to say that history is about us, whether that was meant to suggest how great we are or how depraved. It decenters things, which can be all to the good, since there can be few less productive exercises than debating who is really the Middle Kingdom, or the Shining City on a Hill, and who are the mere pretenders. A decentered perspective delivers us from that folly. Moreover, if we are agile, it can put us onto an alternative way of thinking about the multitudes of cases of people doing this and that carried down to us in history, mythology, literature, and tradition. Instead of trying to figure out how to shoehorn this or that into a plotline that glorifies or condemns the outcome, we have the liberty to take them on their own terms. Or if that seems implausible, we have the liberty to take them on a variety of terms, seeing how that might fit into this or that plotline. In so doing we will develop the interpretive skills, the abilities of reading and construing human action, that we might have hoped for in undertaking college in the first place. Instead of constructing fables, we can construct our own capacities of assessing them and of deconstructing them when necessary. The subject matter is, after all, not the Greeks, for instance, but ourselves.

You may be forgiven for thinking that I just argued that history isn't about us, until it is. Let me be clear. The history we study isn't about us, but the study of history is. The second opportunity arises from our reasonable conviction that the liberal arts in some way constitute an underpinning for democratic culture. This conviction is, arguably, a dominant feature of the "grand narrative" of higher education in America. It turns up among the Founders in Jefferson's founding of the University of Virginia, Adams's writings in support of public education in Massachusetts, and the rising affirmation of the Texas Declaration of Independence, from 1835, that "it is an axiom in political science that unless a people are educated and enlightened it is idle to expect the continuance of civil liberty or the capacity for self-government."

Suppose this is true and suppose also that we have an interest in the growth of democracy across the globe. One of the lessons, surely, of the last decade of American foreign policy is that it is naive and futile to expect democratic institutions to take root in cultures lacking the social and intellectual infrastructure to nourish them. Some of the preconditions of democracy are, no doubt, economic, and some have to do with freedom from a Hobbesian war of all upon all. But some of them, quite likely, also pertain to a complex of implicit cultural understandings and perpetuated habits of thought and practice.

To the extent that such a complex is embedded in the context and practice of the liberal arts, we have to ask what it is about that style and manner of education that makes it useful in this way, and if we can isolate an answer to that question, we have to ask another. That further question is this, posed in awareness of the ignorance, excesses, and arrogance of an age of imperialism and missionary zeal: How, if at all, can we export the benefits of the liberal arts in grounding democratic culture? This question forces us to ask what is essential and what is accidental. If it is true that Western democracy emerged from Enlightenment views about human nature, coupled with capitalism and the rise of a vibrant bourgeoisie, aided by new confidence in the reliability of scientific knowledge, and revulsion over the seventeenth century's wars of religion—or some such confluence of factors—how much of this must be absorbed and indwelled, as is, and by whom, in order to lay the groundwork for democracy in another setting?

Or shall we suppose that the task is not to replicate or inculcate the lessons of the West but to find abroad parallel versions that will lay analogous groundwork in local terms? Can we find liberal education in the Egyptian bureaucratic texts that were used to train officials to govern for the pharaohs? We know these texts as the biblical book of Proverbs. Can we find it in the works of Confucius and Mencius? Or shall we adopt the well-said remark "If it's not your problem, it's unlikely you have the solution"? The trouble with the absolution offered by that remark is that the whole point of globalization is that it's all everyone's problem. We are not free to ignore the social, economic, and political upheavals of far-off places. Nor can we impose solutions. Nor do we know, very well, how to ask in generally acceptable terms what would count as a suitable way of working through the patterns of compromise, mutual accommodation, and outright change that would become a path toward understanding.

What we do know is that acknowledging this list of problems obliges us to confront the way in which we succeed or fail in living up to the very principles we would encourage other people to adopt. I wrote above that the idea that the liberal arts are the underpinning of democracy is part of the grand narrative of higher education in America. Is this a gleam in our eye, or is it a log that occludes our vision as we try to correct others? Several years ago Kate Will, then president of Gettysburg College, referred to the problem of "Jellybyism." The allusion is to the long-range philanthropist Mrs. Jellyby of Dickens's *Bleak House,* who devoted her time to organizing meetings, raising funds, and writing letters for settlers on a distant African river, all the while through virtual criminal neglect relegating her own family to hunger, rags, filth, and dispossession. "Charity begins at home" goes the saying, and so perhaps should our attention to the work of liberal education as a bulwark of democracy. If looking into the world turns out to be a mirror that impresses upon us no more than this, even that will be an improvement.

What more salutary effect of exposure to the rest of the world could we hope for than to see ourselves more clearly, or as others see us. What would we see if we looked at the stranglehold of monied interests on congressional campaign funding and hence on legislation? Or the de facto conversion of political power into a salable commodity? Or the flagrant transformation of judicial decisions to serve the ideologies and financial interests of those who appointed the judges? Mrs. Jellyby may have some housekeeping to do here at home, before we wax too keen on the virtues of what we call democracy, for consumption abroad.

L. P. Hartley's novel *The Go-Between* begins with these lines: "The past is a foreign country. They do things differently there." Readers of Ian McEwan's *Atonement* will recognize the problem in giving an account of the past that does justice to one's own memories and the recollections of others while taking account of the sea changes wrought in both by the passage of time and the reworkings of memories over the years. Reworkings that are themselves hardly neutral and respecting in some sense what actually happened. Memory is now understood not to work like a cabinet of paper files that can be consulted and retrieved. Rather, memory is much more like a palimpsest, a document that is reworked and written over every time a memory is recalled.

Let me insert a confession. I am one of those people who can't finish one reading project without beginning another. As a consequence, at any moment I am likely to have four or five books in various stages of completion, and often—this is an unintended consequence of what must be a form of attention deficit disorder—the books take up conversation in my head as I move through them together.

So once I was reading, concurrently, Dickens's *David Copperfield,* Peter Taylor's *A Summons to Memphis,* and Julian Barnes's *The Sense of an Ending.* Two Brits and a southerner, spread out over a century and three quarters. But each is a first-person, autobiographical narration, given from the perspective of a man in late middle age, carried out by a narrator whose unreliability in each case falls in the spectrum between subtle and outrageous, and whose integrity falls on a spectrum between admirably, inquisitively courageous and cravenly self-deceptive. Reading Dickens, Taylor, and Barnes concurrently turned into a seminar of one on the construction of understanding out of the examination of one's past. We all tell stories we are determined to live by. But some of us manage to do so with a resolute though necessarily imperfect integrity, while others among us fall for that most persuasive of intimate deceivers—ourselves.

But back to Hartley's "The past is a foreign country." What this metaphor gives us is the connection—the likeness, the affinity—between our need to situate ourselves in relation to the past, our own past, and the parallel need to situate ourselves in relation to those who do things differently, not because they are in the past, but because they inhabit some contemporary variant of the human condition significantly different from our own.

We readily accept the idea that our own past is critically relevant to our self-understanding. Hartley puts the contemporary on the same footing. We understand ourselves not at all unless we do so in relation to objects of contrast, objects that, in the dialectical play of things, can merge, blend, or remain in continuing contrast with what we are.

It is important to see that this is not incidental to our identity but constitutive of it. Philosophers have been worrying about the nature of memory since St. Augustine, at least. At least since David Hume we have been attuned to the role of memory in establishing personal identity. Now, in our popular culture, everything from movies like *Fight Club, Total Recall,* and *The Matrix* to our worries about Alzheimer's presents us with vivid reminders that who we think we are—indeed, who we are in fact—is critically dependent on this strange, poorly understood system we call remembering.

In an analogous way, who we in fact are is critically dependent on our relations with others—both as individuals in relation to other people around us and also as a society in relation to other societies, cultures, and human communities. We have Margaret Thatcher to thank for the brilliantly mistaken aperçu that "there is no such thing as society." That's like saying there's no such thing as the human body, since any human body can always be broken down into its constituent systems, parts, pieces, and elements. There is no such thing as society if your criterion for being real is that it correspond to one of the hard, indestructible atoms that have fascinated philosophers from Democritus and Lucretius to Russell and Wittgenstein. But that atom is an imaginative construct, not a given criterion of reality. The fact that there are innumerable ways of imaging societies, their boundaries, and their differences, and that these cut across one another as forms of analysis, is evidence of the complexity of our projects of understanding, not an indication that there is nothing there. Differences are real. Societies are real. It is up to us to decide which ones to attend to and what to make of them.

Much has been made over the last few years of important work by Martha Nussbaum and Anthony Appiah on these issues of the desirability of global citizenship and the cultivation of cosmopolitan identity and perspective. Their work, along with that of Amartya Sen on justice and Michael Sandel on the structures of a just society, deserves attention. Reaching further back we can attend to Adam Smith (more worshipped than read as the author of *The Wealth of Nations*) and his enduring classic *The Theory of Moral Sentiments* and to David Hume, famous for his devastating critique of facile empiricism and his searching analyses of evidence and authority in religion, who also did profoundly important work, in his *A Treatise of Human Nature,* on the capacities of imagination and the resource of sympathy.

With such works as these in mind, let me suggest that the most important aspect of the process of globalization may well be the expanded field it offers for the pursuit and cultivation of sympathetic imagination. Here's the case for that. We see in every account of the benefits of liberal education something about the development of the powers of critical thinking. Even in the narrowest sense, critical thinking is an important ability. Analysis of arguments, evaluation of evidence, and command of the principles of logic, argument, and rhetoric are all important outcomes. But the best and toughest work comes when disagreement arrives at the point where what one party admits as decisive evidence for some momentous conclusion the other party deems insufficient or even irrelevant. That's the point we come up against when we can't see how people apparently as fully human as we are could possibly accept the reasons they do for the conclusions they reach. This is the point where logic gives way to something very much like aesthetics.

This is also the point where carrying forward the effort to understand others—and even more the effort to understand ourselves—demands large capacities of sympathetic imagination. You have to be able to see how the person could "take" the facts as warranting the conclusion she reaches. You have to be able to get some critical distance on the fact that you yourself are "taking" some things as reasons that others find outrageous or beside the point. Socrates said that the whole game was about the maxim "Know thyself." To do that takes more than critical acuity, more than analysis, more than cleverness. It takes imagination and sympathy. It takes an admission that knowing oneself requires an earnest, laborious comparison with other ways of being and thinking. It involves intentional cultivation of a range of sensibilities to which the market does not, of itself, direct us.

So let's hope that the grand irony of globalization can be avoided. Let's evade the great flattening of diversity into trivial difference. Rather than permitting the bounty of a globalized perspective to magnify the chaos of inexplicable, incommensurable preference, let's maintain our grip on the process of learning to choose well. We can do that to the extent that we keep our eye on the main purpose. What happened in history is not about us, but the point of our studying it is very much about us. History matters because knowing it shapes us—and ignoring it shapes us even more. How the rest of the world lives on the earth, thinks, talks, structures society, creates art and wealth, and so on, is not actually about us. But the point of our studying those things is about us. And if how we live—whether well or poorly, whether in praiseworthy ways or in ways that merit scorn—matters, then how we approach them matters just as much. This dimension of the project of the liberal arts is not a frill, not a decoration. It is as serious as the difference between war and peace, between justice and exploitation, or between there being or not being a future.

THWARTED INTENTIONS AND CONFLICT

Woodrow Wilson is often credited with the remark that "academic politics are so bitter because so little is at stake." This remark is ironic on two levels. At the superficial level, the irony lies in the misfit between the terrific intensity of academic disputes over—say, curriculum—and the trifling consequences of decisions one way or the other. But at a deeper level, there is irony in the fact that the remark is deeply false, a fact to which its witty surface blinds us.

By "academic politics" I understand not so much disputes about faculty pay, teaching load, nonteaching governance responsibilities, gender and racial equity, and so forth—though these are extremely important—but the disputes about teaching itself, modes of learning, subjects to be studied, and the curriculum in general. What shall be asked of students, and to what end? Academic politics are so bitter—in this sense—because what is at stake is something close to the meaning of life. And because we disagree about various items in this list, we also seem to be disagreeing about fundamental questions such as "Is life worth living?" or "How can we approach meaning in life?"

This opposition creates a mutual opposition of a particular sort, a sort described by Thomas Hardy in *The Woodlanders,* chapter 7:

> They went noiselessly over mats of starry moss, rustled through interspersed tracts of leaves, skirted trunks with spreading roots, whose mossed rinds made them like hands wearing green gloves; elbowed old elms and ashes with great forks, in which stood pools of water that overflowed on rainy days, and ran down their stems in green cascades. On older trees still than these, huge lobes of fungi grew like lungs. Here, as everywhere, the Unfulfilled Intention, which makes life what it is, was as obvious as it could be among the depraved crowds of a city slum. The leaf was deformed, the curve was crippled, the taper was interrupted; the lichen eat the vigor of the stalk, and the ivy slowly strangled to death the promising sapling.[3]

Here Hardy expresses a dark vision of the competitiveness of life, a competition in which each participant's success is thwarted—that is, crossed and blocked—by the activities of others. Academic politics is like that, in that what one party advocates is often incompatible with what another advocates. And the reasons for advocacy are often unknowable, negligible, or unintelligible from the other perspective.

George Eliot, in her novel *Adam Bede,* offers an illustration of the unintelligibility of the grounds of an opinion. The title character is being advised by his unlearned mother of the affection held for him by the Methodist "preacher lady," Dinah, an affection of which Adam professes ignorance:

> "What dost say such things for, mother, when thee'st got no foundation for 'em? Thee knows nothing as gives thee a right to say that."
>
> "Then I know nought as gi'es me a right to say as the year's turned, for all I feel it fust thing when I get up i' th' mornin'."[4]

Their exchange continues as Adam's mother tells him of inarticulate subtleties of behavior, glances, and turns of expression she has noticed. Adam at length comes to see that his mother has picked up on something he had not: that Dinah loves him. And her grounds for her belief are vague, accumulating gradually and barely noticed, like the change of seasons.

The mutual antagonism of purposes, added to the mutual elusiveness of grounds, makes each perspective look, from the opposing perspective, not merely like error, but more like perversity, even intentional wickedness. Those who disagree are not making mistakes but doing something like blaspheming. And that is why academic politics are so bitter, because they cut to what is most central for us—the meaning of our lives.

6

LIBERAL ARTS AND PERSONAL IDENTITY

IN THIS CHAPTER I argue that our identity as persons who are continuous over time, is contingent on memories, cast and recast in the context of repetitive experiences. These memories, while staying the same or nearly the same in content, are received by us with sensibilities changed by intervening experience. Repeated exposure to and engagement with paradigmatic texts can offer measures of our changes while affirming our continuity. Thus the liberal arts provide a set of experiences that can exhibit the continuity of our personal identity through change. These are matters that affect all of us, not just college undergraduates and their teachers but lifelong learners of all sorts. I will draw on the contrasting stories of Homer's Odysseus and Aeschylus's Agamemnon, on Wordsworth's explicit narrative of this process in "Tintern Abbey," and on Nietzsche's insistence on the interconnectedness of things through his teaching of "eternal recurrence." The argument will both exhibit and exemplify this process.

ODYSSEUS AND AGAMEMNON

"My wife is nothing compared to you for beauty. . . . She is mortal, you are immortal and never grow old. But even so, I long for the day of my homecoming."[1] So Odysseus explains to the goddess, Calypso, his preference for Ithaca and Penelope, home and wife, above a life of immortal delights with her on the island of Ogygia. Calypso offers him fine food and drink, games, leisure, the pleasures of her bed, and the ultimate boon of immortality. But he spends his time, what he has left of it after eating, drinking, and making love with the goddess, staring out to sea toward home, weeping bitter tears and complaining of his sorrow to the waves.

Odysseus had left for the war at Troy as a young man, when his only child was a baby and his wife in the bloom of youth. At the time of the action narrated in *The Odyssey* he is twenty years older, at an ambiguous age. At times he can appear to be the strong, bushy-haired young man ready for athletic games. But he can also appear to be the man nearly past his prime, beginning to wane physically, learning to rely on his cleverness. The facts of human mortality, evidenced by the passing of youth, are clear and immediate. He is aware, too, of the aging of Penelope. He anticipates that on his return she will still be beautiful, but only after the fashion of mortal women, and in the fading way her age allows. With Calypso's offer, and Penelope's faithfulness, Odysseus has a choice of lives and mates. He can choose the eternal enjoyment of an enchanted isle or a return to a scruffy island, an undistinguished land. Homer tells us that Ithaca is goat country, lacking pastures fit for horses. Odysseus chooses homely provenance, an aging wife, a foreseeable tangle of intrigues and battle to regain his home, and, ultimately, death, instead of endless life, youth, and pleasure. Why?

I used to raise this question annually while reading *The Odyssey* in a seminar of first-year students. There is irony in the way our culture consigns classics to the young. Because we suppose that the classics convey great truths, we present them that the young may learn, "privileging them," as Thomas Fuller wrote, "with the experience of age without weathering the infirmities or the inconveniences thereof."[2] But is there a case to be made that the experience of age cannot be gained without the aging itself and the experiences it affords? I began to suspect so when, at the age of thirty-five, I first read Aeschylus's *Agamemnon* with my first-year students. Let me draw together some elements of Agamemnon's story. The great king of the Argives is doomed; the Fates supply five or six independently sufficient reasons for this death. He has sacrificed his daughter Iphigenia for a favorable wind; he outrages decency by bringing Cassandra home cowering under his robe; Clytemnestra and her lover, Aegisthus, need his death to secure their betrayal; Aegisthus needs his death to avenge the deaths of his brothers, cooked in a stew by Agamemnon's father, Atreus; and finally, Agamemnon challenges the gods by treading on a purple carpet. Like a neurotic symptom stemming from a number of independent sources, his death is overdetermined. But beyond its moral necessity, which anyone can appreciate, the death of Agamemnon disclosed a numinous sense giving us a glimpse into the dark life of things. When Clytemnestra, dripping blood, rolls out his body on a cart, she cries,

> So he went down
> Life pumping out of him
> And gurgling murderous spurts of blood
> Which enlivened me with a black-ensanguined drizzle
> Oh, it freshened me like drops from heaven
> When the earth is bright and sprung with budding.
>
> (ll. 1410–15)

On reading this passage aloud during a discussion, I found myself in the midst of an epiphany: I saw Agamemnon's death as a ritual sacrifice. He is killed in his homecoming bath, the murder weapon concealed in a welcoming robe. Like a great bull marked for sacrifice, he crumples beneath the knife, betrayed by his own wife. Clytemnestra's bath of life in Agamemnon's blood displayed to me a dark connection. While he dies, she is freshened by the bloody drops. He pours out vitality and is emptied; she becomes the fertile earth, flourishing with life and growth through his death. A horribly thrilling realization of the linkages among love, sex, reproduction, and death washed over me as I stood before the class. It is the way of epiphanies to be intense and private. While I pulsed with the sensual charge of discovering what Aeschylus had shown, the seminar members sat quietly puzzled at my overreaction, as they saw it, to a few lines of rather lurid poetry. No explanations could diminish the privacy of my experience. Only years, and experiences of the right sort, could let them in on the secret.

At eighteen, none of my students had a spouse or children or a marriage to lose to a usurper. Whatever their experience of sex, none of them could have had the long years of constancy with a spouse that displays its bonding powers. None of them knew from the perspective of one who has a spouse, a home, and children, about the power, the complexity, and the ambivalences of the webbing that links women and men on the brink of middle age to these dimensions of their identities. Even at thirty-five, I did know, and Aeschylus's depiction struck like Clytemnestra's knife. At eighteen, they did not, and the picture passed them by. I deserved no credit for my insight, and they deserved no blame. I was thirty-five, and they were not. And I was trying to lead them to relish a classic whose power they could feel only later, after much more life. The irony of trying to teach the young about life is this: we who teach are the ones who learn.

And yet our efforts are not wasted. Every college teacher has experienced the encounter with the matured former student who says: "You know, I never understood until just last year what you meant in Intro to Philosophy when you said . . ." These experiences are both gratifying and unsettling. For my own part, I seldom remember having said it at all, much less whatever worth ruminating on for a decade I might have meant by it. But this awkwardness aside, such anecdotal evidence fits well with the received notion that liberal arts students mature, in the years following graduation, into an appreciation of what they hear and do as undergraduates. So perhaps leading eighteen-year-olds into engagement with Odysseus and Agamemnon is not wasted after all, despite the privacy of our epiphanies.

WORDSWORTH: REPETITION AND CONTINUANCE

It may be that what is happening in the scene above with my student is suggested by William Wordsworth in "Tintern Abbey":

> While here I stand, not only with the sense
> Of present pleasure, but with pleasing thoughts
> That in this moment there is life and food
> For future years.
>
> (ll. 62–65)

On such occasions as the one I have described, the best, deepest present pleasure is ours as mature learners, but if the process works, the life and food for future years can be the undergraduates' as well. We say that liberal education shapes the feelings and trains the sensibilities. By exploring more deeply these lines of Wordsworth's, we may be able to see more clearly how that happens, and in so doing then move toward an understanding of Odysseus's choice. And by understanding that choice we will also come to understand more fully how it is that reading and teaching the same texts, again and again, over a period of years can produce a rich weave of remembrance and can help, in fact, to constitute an identity. The route to an appreciation of Odysseus's decision will lead us through two strains of thought—perhaps an unlikely pair. We will first consider Wordsworth on the significance of repeated experiences set in the changing circumstances of our lives, and then look at Friedrich Nietzsche on the moral challenge posed by an awareness that those experiences constitute us as ourselves in connection with a world of chance and transition. Finally, I will show the link between Odysseus's choice and what we can come to know through the slow lessons of reading and teaching, over and over, during many years, the same texts. Seeing this, we see that in doing so we are not only teaching about but also, through teaching, actually living lives of human significance.

Wordsworth writes in the preface to *Lyrical Ballads* (1800) that poetry "takes its origin from emotion recollected in tranquility."[3] It is a truism to observe that Wordsworth's work is often about the recollected experiences of the poet and even about the process of writing poetry as a device for constructing a relation among several mutually interdefining elements—the poet, his experience of a phenomenon, the feeling thereby generated, and the further use of the experience in memory to generate morally useful emotions. In "Tintern Abbey," Wordsworth complicates this basic structure by narrating a return visit to the scene of earlier emotions. The ingredients described above remain intact but are layered over with the emotional consequences of a second experience.

The poet has returned to the Wye after long absence, and in the poem he sets off to construct relations within and between two sets of elements. One set, the first layer, comprises the memory of the phenomenon, the poet remembered by himself as what he then was, the emotion remembered as originally experienced, and the remembered past uses of the experience as remembered, the emotions it had generated, and their role in the intervening life of the poet. A second, parallel layer comprises the phenomenon as reexperienced, the poet perceived by himself as changed from what he was, the contemporary emotion experienced in contrast to the emotion as remembered from the original experience, and the remembered uses of the original experience in complement and contrast to the anticipated further uses of future memories of the contemporary experience.

I believe that this complex structure is worth making explicit because it adumbrates steps in a recursive process in which repeated experiences preserve, incorporate, and reinterpret their predecessors. One gets the flavor of this process by recalling that Wordsworth's composition of "Tintern Abbey" involves the initial visit, the second visit with its memories of the first, and the occasion of composition itself, involving both memories of the second visit (with its embedded memories) and of the first. In this process, complicated but not impenetrable or disorderly relationships develop among layers of experience and emotion both immediate and remembered. Because these relationships exist among related versions—changed over time and reinterpreted—of what are in some sense the same things, the relationships' development can be considered a kind of layering of memory, feeling, and sensibility. By "sensibility" I mean the capacity of the person to be affected by feelings upon having or remembering certain experiences. Layering is an important notion because our sensibilities will grow, diminish, or simply change, and the experience of our old capacities to be affected with feelings will coexist in memory with our new and different sensibilities. Simultaneously, both are related as past and present versions of ourselves, incorporating the same memories interpreted differently at different layers.

In "Tintern Abbey," Wordsworth recalls a set of vanished sensibilities—those that shaped a youthful, unreflective absorption into Nature—and says,

—That time is past,
And all its aching joys are now no more,
And all its dizzy raptures.

(ll. 83–85)

Those sensibilities are lost but not forgotten. Wordsworth does not regret their loss, since they have been displaced by deeper, richer sensibilities whose very depth and richness consists in their incorporation of an appreciation of just those vanished capacities for being affected by experience, and in his understanding that those later sensibilities are developments out of and away from the earlier ones. He has, he writes, "abundant recompense" (l. 88). In so far as our sense of self emerges through a consideration of such transparencies, we come to see ourselves as a deeply layered palimpsest, imperfectly erased at every depth, rewritten in successive layers around persisting and evolving themes.

Wordsworth describes this rewriting in general terms in the preface to *Lyrical Ballads:* "Our continual influxes of feeling are modified and directed by our thoughts, which are indeed the representatives of all our past feelings, and . . . by contemplating the relation of these general representatives to each other, we discover what is really important to men."[4] Intrinsic to this process is a regularity of repetition in changed circumstances, a habit Wordsworth calls "repetition and continuance."

Of what utility in understanding Odysseus's choice are these reflections on Wordsworth and the repetitive layering of experience and feeling in the evolution of oneself? Before addressing this question directly, let us route our inquiry through a consideration of Friedrich Nietzsche's teaching of eternal recurrence.

NIETZSCHE AND THE INTERCONNECTEDNESS OF THINGS

In *Thus Spoke Zarathustra* (1892) and other works, Nietzsche propounds a doctrine of "eternal recurrence" (*das ewige Wiederkehr*). The doctrine holds that everything that happens recurs infinitely. The cosmos is an infinitely repetitive cycle, in which every event must happen as it does because precisely that event has already occurred infinitely many times in the past and will occur again infinitely many times in the future. Commentators have debated whether Nietzsche's claim is an earnest assertion about the nature of the cosmos. But no reader of Nietzsche doubts that the main import of the doctrine is moral. How does one respond to the (purported) fact that this life—in every detail—has been and will be lived over and over again, world without end? Does one say "yes" or "no" to life so conceived?

This difficult teaching has been subject to several interpretations. By way of comparison, let us consider a familiar myth. Sisyphus, because he disclosed Zeus's whereabouts in one of the god's trysts with mortal women, is condemned to an endless task of excruciating boredom and futility. He must roll a huge rock up the slope of a mountain from whose summit it immediately rolls down, ready to be pushed up again. And so on eternally. Albert Camus has made the myth a celebrated image of courage and good cheer in the face of hopeless absurdity: "One must imagine Sisyphus happy."[5] My object is not to defend Camus's Sisyphus, the existentialist hero, but to note that Camus takes as his premise the horror of an activity that is endlessly repetitious, intrinsically burdensome, and fundamentally absurd. According to Brenda Magnus's reading, this is also the premise of Nietzsche's eternal recurrence. Let us ask whether it fits Odysseus's choice. Magnus argues that "eternal recurrence is to be regarded . . . as an existential imperative. . . . Existence itself is to be regarded '*sub specie eternitatis*.'"[6] Eternal recurrence intensifies—by eternalizing—the content of experience and asks for a response of joyous affirmation to the notion that this, exactly *this*, recurs infinitely.

When we think of Ogygia under the challenge of eternal recurrence, its threat seems to be the boredom of endless sameness. But we face a crucial disanalogy with Sisyphus. Sisyphus is laboring with a rock; Odysseus is distorting himself with a goddess. We are faced with an interpretation of Odysseus as a man who simply cannot sit still, not even for a good thing. Indeed, this interpretation turns up in Tennyson's "Ulysses," where the old king has come to see Ithaca as merely a domestic Ogygia and pushes off in search of new worlds and new adventures. When we bear these considerations in mind, Odysseus's choice seems hard to scrutinize through the lenses of eternal recurrence. He seems to flee from it, not to embrace it, and that which he flees is intrinsically delightful, or—at least in Tennyson's case—intrinsically good. If we suppose that the delightful and the good have somehow cloyed, Odysseus simply flees the unbearable—hardly a morally instructive action. If we suppose that Calypso still delights him, we must understand Odysseus to be rejecting something wonderful in favor of something mundane—an odd choice but still not morally instructive.

Something important is lost in this reading of Odysseus's choice. Nietzsche's Zarathustra calls eternal recurrence his "most abysmal thought"[7] and in *The Will to Power* Nietzsche calls it "most terrible" and "the extremist form of nihilism."[8] What is most terrible, abysmal, and nihilistic about eternal recurrence is the idea that the Übermensch's overcoming of the "small man" is not a final victory. Zarathustra says, "The great disgust with man—*this* choked me. . . . Alas, man recurs eternally. The small man recurs eternally!"[9] So Nietzsche's doctrine is not merely a challenge to accept the threats of eternal sameness and repetition but to accept the cycles of origin and decline that typify human lives. Odysseus's leaving Calypso signifies a loyalty to humanity—to the inexorable patterns of birth, maturity, and death in whose context alone we can recognize a life that we would claim as our own.

Is life with Calypso a human life? Calypso herself is, in a sense, not a person. She is not a character who changes, ages, and will die. She is a cartoon, lacking depth, texture, and the dynamic patterns of development through changing circumstances that is central in human lives. With Calypso there is no layering of experience, just repetitive superimposition of the same, which produces no texture. Life on Ogygia is not fully human. It does not offer the possibility of the continual emergence of a layered, developing self.

The real relevance of Nietzsche's doctrine to the choice can be discovered in a consideration of Alexander Nehamas's construal of eternal recurrence. Nehamas separates its moral import from the dubious thesis about the actual repetition of the cosmic cycle, arguing that "eternal recurrence is not a view of the cosmos but a theory of the self."[10] The core image is vividly expressed in the possibility of repetitious cosmic cycles, in which one's own life precisely recurs, but its real sense lies in a more immediate—and less extravagant—idea. The core idea is a challenge to affirm oneself in a world so thoroughly characterized by the interpenetration and connectedness of things that to affirm a single moment or event is to affirm the totality. Likewise, to reject a single moment or event is to reject the world in its totality. Nehamas writes that according to Nietzsche, "A life that was different in any way simply would not be our life; it would be the life of a different person." And "If I accept any part of myself and my life, then I accept everything about it, and everything about the whole world as well" (*NLL* 156). The central point of eternal recurrence, then, is not a pattern of endless cycles but the close interlocking of everything, including the sequences of actions and experiences that make up human lives, including especially the relationships that define the lives of different persons.

If we think of the doctrine of eternal recurrence as a challenge to accept the interconnectedness of all things in their rhythms of origin and decline, then it becomes significant that there is in Calypso's time with Odysseus the progenitive meaning of the sexual life. And the promise of eternal youth looms as a temptation to separate the activities of eating, drinking, playing, and making love from their networks of human significance. These activities were bereft of the shifting contexts in which they can come to bear, at different times, different meanings. And so they cannot contribute to the process so well mapped out by Wordsworth in which our identities are woven by layering of experiences. The deepest challenge of eternal recurrence is to accept the interconnectedness of things. Whether or not we accept Nietzsche's view that everything that happens is implicated in each single event, the facts of our lives are such that powerful patterns of connections weave a fabric. Ogygia is an island, insular, unconnected. Life there is rootless, deracinated from all that in a human life lies before, after, and around each event. Odysseus's choice is loyalty to personhood: to being a person and to living among other persons. Leaving aside the deterministic quandaries posed by eternal recurrence, let us consider Odysseus's choice in terms of the Nietzschean principle that a thing is the totality of its relationships.

Nehamas writes that "for Nietzsche all things in the world are interconnected and . . . their interconnections are essential to their very character" (*NLL* 79). He argues that Nietzsche should be understood as replacing ontology with genealogy. That is "the unity of each thing, that thing itself, is to be found in the genealogical account that connects one set of phenomena with another" (*NLL* 104). Applied to personal identity, this means that "the self is the sum of its acts along with their contents, each self is constituted not simply by the fact *that* it thinks, wants, and acts, but also precisely by *what* it thinks, wants, and does" (*NLL* 180). Insofar, then, as we can talk about unity and coherence in the self, they will be explicable only by reference to the constancy and harmony of the connections that link the self with other selves, with continuing interests and projects, and with institutions, places, and things. The imagery of weaving that is so important in *The Odyssey*—not only Penelope but also Calypso and even Circe are weavers—captures the idea of interconnecting strands and the production of pattern through repetition and change. The genealogy of the self, then, lies in its relations and, more precisely, in the relations between current versions of such relations and their predecessors. One becomes what one is—to use Nietzsche's paradoxical phrase—by a process of emergence by which one's constituent relations evolve into their descendants, and thus the pattern that these make up evolves into a descendant of itself.

Does this account help us in understanding Odysseus's choice? It does if we understand the doctrine of eternal recurrence in the right way. It is not at last a challenge to confront and overcome the challenge of Sisyphean monotony. It is a challenge to embrace and accept another sort of inevitability, the inevitability of one's rootedness in the process of things and one's interconnectedness with the other constituents of that process. Ogygia represents a fantastic refuge from that interconnectedness and so represents an idea of the self as independent, sufficient in itself, held apart from the flux. Ogygia is the fantasy of the self liberated from death. So in choosing Penelope and Ithaca, Odysseus chooses the finitude of the human self with its essential interconnections, its emergent life and its ultimate death.

Opposition, conflict, and death are the dark side of those interconnections. To accept their inevitability is the challenge of eternal recurrence, and Odysseus accepts them for the purpose of affirming those relationships that have made him who he is and will continue to contribute to his becoming who he will be. To remain in Ogygia would be to stop being king in Ithaca, husband to Penelope, father to Telemachus, son to the old king Laertes, grown-up boy to Eurycleia, and lord over the swineherds, goatherds, and warriors. It would mean giving up being a hero of the Trojan War, for wars and battles are a part of the process from which Ogygia is insulated. To remain there would be, in fact, to give up being Odysseus except in name and in a frozen memory that is irrelevant, fixed in its uselessness to the understanding of present experience. Indeed, to stay with Calypso would be to jettison the entire genealogy of the Odysseus who arrived there. By contrast, to go home is to pick up all those relations again—to be sure, on new terms. It is to supply the hero of the Trojan War to complement the reluctant warrior who left. It is to resume the roles supplied by his own past, to celebrate the genealogy that produced him, and to affirm the continuity of becoming who he is in the only way that is humanly possible—namely, by incorporating and building upon his past.

It is important to understand that it is not the mere fact that these connections have existed in Odysseus's past that makes them supremely worth taking up. If that were the case, the moral of the story would simply be the familiar, and often false, opinion that the old, the customary, and the conservative are the best options. Rather, the point is that since these connections have constituted Odysseus's past, they therefore constitute the best and richest point of departure for his future. Odysseus's choice is forward looking, not backward looking. He aims to restore himself in Ithaca, not as he was before leaving, but as he can be having left and having returned. When he meets Penelope, they lie down not as young lovers but as a couple with a history mutually understood, in a bed they knew in youth, whose special significance appears in its role as a link between their past and their present. Odysseus's experience of Penelope, and both their experiences in and out of their bed, exemplify the superimposition of related experiences and the experience of oneself as continuous but changed. On his return Odysseus resumes the layering of experience and the webbing of connectedness that form the continuity of his identity.

The bed is a central image in *The Odyssey.* In the heart of his home, it is the fixed center of centers, kept by Penelope, to which he returns.[11] It is fixed by being literally rooted in the ground; one of its posts Odysseus fashioned from an olive tree, which he left rooted in the soil from which it grew. The import of the bed is clear—connectedness and rootedness, not changelessness but continuity. Thus the bed is not only the literal destination but also the perfect metaphor of Odysseus's choice.

What Odysseus chooses is participation in the process that, in the case of my first-year students, will lead to an understanding of his choice. He chooses to return, to take up a new version of the old pattern, to reexperience the familiar in changed circumstances. In so doing he chooses to come to feel the changes in his own sensibilities, to see his present and future capacities to be affected by experiences as developments out of his previous capacities, and, in all this process, to understand himself as having a personal genealogy that consists of the emergent pattern composed by the continually changing nature of his interconnections with persons, places, things, and institutions.

Students in later life may come—in recollection or rereading—to understand Odysseus's choice or the death of Agamemnon. They will remember their partial youthful comprehension; in so doing they will look back through past and present memories of themselves and will understand themselves as changed in sensibility. Apprehending that change, they will come increasingly to think of themselves as persons knitted into patterns of significance, persons whose lives have histories and whose lives yield and unfold meaning. In the best of circumstances, this process can produce epiphany. Wordsworth writes, again in "Tintern Abbey,"

> While with an eye made quiet by the power
> Of harmony, and the deep power of joy,
> We see into the life of things.
>
> (ll. 47–49)

Liberal education, in its training of the sensibilities, discloses these powers of harmony and joy, and opens lines of sight into "the life of things." Of course the eye is also trained to discern discord and anguish, and no process of becoming oneself is complete without an understanding of that side of the life of things. Agamemnon's murder shows us something to be reckoned with, as surely as Odysseus's homecoming does.

Odysseus's happy homecoming to a waiting wife and his righteous vengeance on the predatory suitors could hardly contrast more sharply with the betrayal of Agamemnon and the triumph of his usurper, Aegisthus. Yet the deep lesson is the same in both: the deep power of connections. Certainly, the nature of the connections is different in the two cases. Agamemnon's story is a tragedy; he willfully chooses that to which he is doomed in any case. Both his virtues and his vices do him in, while Odysseus survives.

If the concept of a "classic" is the idea that it belongs to a community, and that in a community's apprehension of its classics, a community's members sort through and reformulate over and over again the interconnected significances of man and woman, youth and maturity, triumph and tragedy, and all the gradations between. These significances change, and it is the constancy of the exemplars that allows us to see the changes in our apprehension of them—that is, in ourselves. Odysseus and Agamemnon change in our understanding because we change, and it is—among other things—our repetitious acquaintance with them that exhibits our acquaintance with them so vividly. Therein lies the point of reading *The Odyssey,* year after year, with first-year students. Without the reading, or its equivalent, we would become deracinated, as Odysseus himself would have been had he chosen Ogygia and Calypso. Without experiences of repetition and continuance, we will not become changeless and immortal, but we will almost certainly fail to apprehend the changes we undergo in our lives and fail to sense what patterns build there. With the rereading, we can continue the layering of our experience and observe our thorough interconnectedness in the natural rhythms of origin and transition, gaining the opportunity to affirm the changing meanings that accumulate in the process. *The Odyssey* is, for me, an Ithaca to which I can return to learn about my own life, and if there is a joy in reading it with students, it resides in offering it to them in the hope that it might become, for them, such a touchstone.

AFTERWORD

In the various roles we are called upon to play in life, we are generally someone's successor, which means of course that someone is our predecessor. I am grateful that John Churchill was mine. Since the founding in 1883 of the United Chapters of Phi Beta Kappa, the forerunner to today's Phi Beta Kappa Society, there have been only ten secretaries, the title given to the chief executive officer. John was the ninth. When a person dies as suddenly and as unexpectedly as John did, for those of us left behind there is a sense not only of loss but of a conversation interrupted. I know that I am not the only one who experienced this with John's passing. John died shortly before the annual meeting of the Phi Beta Kappa Senate, the society's governing board. It was our custom to speak before Senate meetings, to talk over the issues that we intended to raise that year. "Call John" is still on my "To Do" list, left over from November 2019. I cannot make myself delete the reminder.

In an effort to continue the conversation that has been interrupted, I begin with John's own words, then proceed to some words about John, and finally turn to words that John read and heard. *The Problem with Rules* is the perfect place to begin this effort. The work is based on John's final major lectures, and, being published posthumously, it is literally a continuation of his words and thoughts after death. Moreover, there is a "meta nature" to this project that John would have appreciated. In many ways, *The Problem with Rules* is itself a continuation of a conversation, John's lifelong engagement with Ludwig Wittgenstein. Like this current volume, Wittgenstein's great *Philosophical Investigations* was published posthumously, in 1953, two years after his death. In much of his work, and especially in this volume, John mined *Philosophical Investigations* for a less certain and more profound Wittgenstein than that revealed in the more insistent *Tractatus Logico-Philosophicus* published in 1921 (translated by D. F. Pears and B. F. McGuinness, New York, Humanities Press, 1961). It was to the posthumously published work of his avatar that he turned in this his own posthumous work for an answer to a question he pursued for an entire lifetime: how to understand the nature and aims of a liberal arts and sciences education.

These lectures turned chapters in his final book are very much in the form of a deep conversation with John. Yes, we experience his profound understanding of Wittgenstein, a philosopher whose opacity challenges both novices and experts alike. But we also experience the breadth of John's knowledge base, from the ancients to the moderns, from philosophy and history to fiction and poetry, and from baseball to baking biscuits.

John's ultimate answer to the nature of the liberal arts, through his study of Wittgenstein, began with a lack of certainty in our values, that is, a willingness to challenge every conclusion, no matter how deeply held. There is a correlative commitment to the process by which this challenge takes place.

Liberal education requires of us the acceptance, as John puts it, of the "endlessness of the task of self-examination" (48). The process of endless self-examination may actually require more than just acceptance; it requires a commitment. John suggests that liberal education's "chief aim [is the] disciplined reflection on the emergence of meaning" (50, 66).

The vital importance of self-examination and disciplined reflection is as ancient as Socrates's celebrated defense at his trial for impiety that "the unexamined life is not worth living" (Plato's *Apology*). The value of these bedrock attributes of a liberal education are clear in our time as well. One source that is often looked to today to evaluate curricula or pedagogy are student course evaluations. Of course, there is a limit to what evaluations performed immediately after the conclusion of a class can capture. We would like to know not only what a college student thinks is valuable having just completed a course but also what she or he will look back on years hence as having had enduring value. During John's tenure as secretary of Phi Beta Kappa, just such an experiment was conducted. Groups of long-standing members of Phi Beta Kappa were assembled around the country and asked to considered what they thought to be the greatest benefits of their liberal arts education. Chief among these was the skill of deliberation (57, 83).

Inspired by Wittgenstein's embrace of uncertainty, we can see the purpose of a liberal education as less about the mastery of a given body of material and more about developing an ability to engage deeply and critically with ideas. As John describes it, "Liberal arts is not possession of a settled opinion, but the constant conflict between contenders. It is an activity, not a possession. If genuine deliberation requires a context of mutual vulnerability and generosity, it needs a special context, a context protected from our reflexes of suspicion, self-interest, defensiveness, and favoritism" (72). This notion of liberal education looks both outward and inward. Outward-looking, the activity of working our way through the conflicts among contending theses and arguments helps us come to an understanding of our world. Inward-looking, liberal education provides a set of experiences the interrogation of which permits us to discover our self-identity as it changes through time (chapter 6, passim).

There is something almost Emersonian about the celebration of self-discovery. In addressing the need for liberal education to "accept" globalization, John has a little fun at the expense of the great transcendentalist and early feminist Margaret Fuller, whose expression "I accept the universe!" is supposed to have prompted Thomas Carlyle's rejoinder "Gad! She'd better!" (103). But Fuller herself was the product of just such a liberal education as John has conceived, one that inculcated the ultimate skill of deliberation. Hers was a blend of formal education and self-education. She claimed to have first learned from Emerson "what is meant by an inward life": "Many other springs have since fed the stream of living waters, but he first opened the fountain. That the 'mind is its own place,' was a dead phrase to me, till he cast light upon my mind. Several of his sermons stand apart in memory, like landmarks of my spiritual history. It would take a volume to tell what this one influence did for me" (Letter from Margaret Fuller to William Henry Channing, quoted in Charles Caper, *Margaret Fuller: An America Romantic Life,* 216, Oxford University Press).

I suspect John would also have been pleased with the support he could draw from the great early and mid-twentieth century jurist Learned Hand. Hand's words in his stirring "The

Spirit of Liberty" address in 1944 retain particular relevance to our time and to John's project as accepting uncertainty in values but demanding commitment to endless examination: "The spirit of liberty is the spirit which is not too sure that it is right; the spirit of liberty is the spirit which seeks to understand the minds of other men and women; the spirit of liberty is the spirit which weighs their interest alongside its own without bias."

John's focus on deliberation was clearly on his mind as he began his term as secretary of Phi Beta Kappa. In his first column in our quarterly *Key Reporter,* he wrote eloquently about the surprisingly complex structure of the Phi Beta Kappa Society, today composed of 290 campus-based chapters, nearly 50 community-based alumni associations, and the national office based in Washington, DC. This structure led him to focus on the importance of deliberative democracy in our lives, our institutions, and our society. He wrote,

> My hope . . . in taking office as Secretary of the Phi Beta Kappa Society, is to maintain and even improve the context of that deliberation, to assist all of our constituencies in maneuvering the complexities of our governance and, above all, to heighten the influence of Phi Beta Kappa and our ideals in the public life of this country and the world, both within academe and in the broader culture. . . . I am [also] conscious that those historical gavels [of Phi Beta Kappa to be used at Senate meetings] are not mine to wield. The Secretary's implement is the pen. I will use it. (Phi Beta Kappa *Key Reporter,* Winter 2002)

As secretary he wrote and spoke widely in support of the liberal arts and sciences. John expanded the reach of the Phi

Beta Kappa Society, twice served with distinction as chair of the board of the National Humanities Alliance, and launched the National Arts and Sciences Initiative.

Fifteen years later, in his final secretary's column in *Key Reporter,* he set out his motivation for his highly successful secretaryship but also for all of us—those who came before going back to 1883 and those who will follow: "We who have been the heads of this organization over the decades, or centuries, are motivated to write and speak in support of the arts and sciences because Phi Beta Kappa has a unique responsibility toward the core disciplines and values that animate American higher education" (Phi Beta Kappa *Key Reporter,* Spring 2016). It was fortuitous that in the same issue, indeed on the page facing John's column, was a "Member Spotlight" on Cornel West. West is quoted as saying: "None of us alone can save the nation or the world. But each of us can make a positive difference if we commit ourselves to do so." Unlikely planned, West's wisdom serves as a fitting summary of John's term as secretary.

When John retired, his colleagues presented him with a respectful and loving resolution of tribute:

> The Team at 1606 New Hampshire proudly and affectionately recognizes John Churchill, Secretary of The Phi Beta Kappa Society as an inspirational and kind leader, a pillar of Phi Beta Kappa knowledge and lore, an accomplished story teller and poet, elocutionist extraordinaire (of Wittgenstein quotes in particular, in German no less), a serious Nats fan, beloved friend of nature, except for squirrels, and a true Southern gentleman.

Your exemplary dedication to the highest ideals of the liberal arts and sciences—breadth of knowledge, critical inquiry, and the pursuit of wisdom—is greatly appreciated by all of your staff.

It is hard to think about John and not smile. He was a philosopher of the first rank, but he wore his erudition lightly and mixed it with both humor and warmth. He was an Oxford- and Yale-educated philosopher who proudly held a blue ribbon for his pickled okra. Perhaps it was all best captured by his broad, deep, all-encompassing laugh that was thoroughly and delightfully contagious.

Having shared John's words, and then words about John, it is right to conclude with words that John surely must have read. It is Wittgenstein's observation on death in *Tractatus Logico-Philosophicus:* "Death is not an event in life: we do not live to experience death. If we take eternity to mean not infinite temporal duration but timelessness, then eternal life belongs to those who live in the present. Our life has no end in the way in which our visual field has no limits."

The citation that the Phi Beta Kappa staff presented to John upon his retirement as quoted above is incomplete. The final words of the resolution were: "You will be missed, but never forgotten." I do not understand these words only in the sense of pleasant memories of a lost friend. To be never forgotten is to be part of a continuing conversation, however interrupted literally by death. To be remembered in this sense is to be someone whose works, words, and thoughts are a place to which one returns.

This volume concludes with an insight I heard from John on several occasions. The experience of reading classic works is that of developing a set of texts to which one can return again and again, developing and revealing our sense of ourselves. And the experience of teaching classic works to students is that of seeking to provide them which such benchmarks for their lives.

> *The Odyssey* is, for me, an Ithaca to which I can return to learn about my own life, and if there is a joy in reading it with students, it resides in offering it to them in the hope that it might become, for them, such a touchstone. (134)

We are each other's Ithacas, and in our relationships we share words to which others might return, not only to remember us, but to learn about their own lives.

In the various roles we are called upon to play in life, someone is our predecessor. I am grateful that John Churchill was mine.

RESOLUTION OF THE PHI BETA KAPPA SENATE IN MEMORY OF DR. JOHN HUGH CHURCHILL (1949–2019)

Whereas John Hugh Churchill was the ninth secretary of the Phi Beta Kappa Society, serving with great distinction from 2001 to 2016; and

Whereas his tenure was marked by his exemplary dedication to the highest ideals of the liberal arts and sciences—breadth of knowledge, critical inquiry, and the pursuit of wisdom; and

Whereas he served as an inspirational and kind leader, a pillar of Phi Beta Kappa knowledge and lore, an accomplished storyteller and poet, and a source of joyful exuberance; and

Whereas during his tenure, he oversaw the creation of the National Arts and Sciences Initiative and of the Secretary's Circle major donor program, strengthened support for chapter and association officers, guided the society successfully through two economic recessions, reimagined the national headquarters of the society, bringing it to 1606 New Hampshire Avenue, and established long-lasting relationships with peer organizations; and

Whereas in 2018, he was honored at the Triennial Council, where he graciously accepted the Phi Beta Kappa President's Award in recognition of his truly outstanding and extraordinary service to Phi Beta Kappa as a national organization;

Now therefore the Senate of the Phi Beta Kappa Society hereby records its profound respect and deep affection for John Hugh Churchill for his service to the Phi Beta Kappa Society.

FREDERICK M. LAWRENCE
SECRETARY AND CEO, THE PHI BETA KAPPA SOCIETY,
AND DISTINGUISHED LECTURER, GEORGETOWN
UNIVERSITY LAW CENTER

NOTES

PREFACE

1. Soren Kierkegaard, *Soren Kierkegaard's Journals and Papers*, ed. and trans. Howard V. Hong and Edna H. Hong (Bloomington: Indiana University Press, 1967), 4:164.

1. THE "ESSENCE" OF LIBERAL EDUCATION

1. Frederick J. Streng, *Emptiness: A Study in Religious Meaning* (Nashville: Abingdon Press, 1967), 220.
2. Overview: History of the Gifford Lectures, https://www.giffordlectures.org/overview.
3. William James, *The Varieties of Religious Experience* (New York: Modern Library, New York, 1902), 27. Hereafter cited parenthetically as *VRE*.
4. Ludwig Wittgenstein, *Philosophical Investigations*, trans. and ed. G. E. M. Anscombe (New York: Macmillan, 1958), §65ff. Hereafter cited parenthetically by section (§) as *PI*.
5. Ray Monk, *Wittgenstein: The Duty of Genius* (New York: Free Press, 1990), 51, 122.
6. Ibid., 478.
7. Francis Bacon, *Novum Organum*, in *The English Philosophers from Bacon to Mill*, ed. E. A. Burtt (New York: Modern Library, 1939), 42.

8. René Descartes, "Discourse on Method," in *The European Philosophers from Descartes to Nietzsche,* ed. Monroe C. Beardsley (New York: Modern Library, 1960), 6.
9. Martin Gardener, ed., *More Annotated Alice: Alice's Adventures in Wonderland and through the Looking Glass* (1990).
10. Walt Whitman, "Song of Myself," in *Leaves of Grass* (New York: Modern Library, 1993), 33.
11. Aristotle, *Nicomachean Ethics* (Indianapolis: Bobbs-Merrill, 1993), 61.

2. WITTGENSTEIN ON RULES AND ITS RELEVANCE FOR LIBERAL EDUCATION

1. Ludwig Wittgenstein, "A Lecture on Ethics," *Philosophical Review,* January 1965.
2. Bertrand Russell, "Some Philosophical Contacts," in *Portraits from Memory,* (New York: Clarion Books), 23.
3. Brian McGuinness, *Wittgenstein: A Life,* vol. 1, *Young Wittgenstein, 1889–1921* (Berkeley: University of California Press, 1988), 118.
4. Leonard Woolf, *The Journey Not the Arrival Matters: An Autobiography of the Years 1939 to 1969* (London: Hogarth, 1969), 48.
5. Monk, *Wittgenstein,* 256.
6. David Edmonds and John Eidinow, *Wittgenstein's Poker* (New York: Ecco, 1990), 194.
7. Matthew Bevis, "I Can Bite Anything I Want," *London Review of Books,* July 16, 2015.
8. Blaise Pascal, Thoughts, #72, "Man's Disproportion," in *The European Philosophers from Descartes to Nietzsche,* ed. Monroe C. Beardsley (New York: Modern Library, 1960), 99–103.
9. David Hume, *A Treatise of Human Nature,* book 1, part 3, sections 5–8, ed. L. A. Selby-Bilge (Oxford: Oxford University Press, 1951).

10. Robert Pirsig, *Zen and the Art of Motorcycle Maintenance* (New York: Morrow, 1974).
11. Lewis Carroll, "What the Tortoise Said to Achilles," *Mind*, 1895.
12. Louie, "Baking Grandma's Bread," https://www.traditionaloven.com/46/how-grandma-baked-delicious-breads.
13. Ludwig Wittgenstein, *On Certainty*, ed. G. E. M. Anscombe and G. H. Von Wright, trans. Denis Paul and G. E. M. Anscombe (Oxford: Basil Blackwell, 1969), §139. Hereafter cited parenthetically by section (§) as *OC*.
14. Ludwig Wittgenstein, *Zettel*, ed. G. E. M. Anscombe and G. H. Von Wright, trans. G. E. M. Anscombe (Oxford: Basil Blackwell, 1967), 391. Hereafter cited parenthetically by section (§) as *Z*.

3. BENEFITS OF LIBERAL EDUCATION

1. James Boswell, *The Life of Samuel Johnson, L.L.D.* (New York, Modern Library, n.d.), 535.
2. Scott Bombay, "Surveys: Many Americans Know Little about the Supreme Court," National Constitution Center, February 17, 2016, https://constitutioncenter.org/blog/surveys-many-americans-know-little-about-the-supreme-court/.
3. Michael Hayden, "The End of Intelligence," *New York Times*, April 29, 2018.
4. George Eliot, "Essay on Thomas Carlyle," *The Leader*, October 27, 1855, reprinted in *Essays of George Eliot*, ed. Thomas Pinney (New York: Oxford University Press, 1963), 213.
5. Kenneth Grahame, *The Wind in the Willows* (New York: Holt, Rinehart, and Winston, 1980), 5.
6. Graham Chapman et al., *The Complete Monty Python's Flying Circus: All the Words* (New York: Pantheon Books, 1989), 86–88.
7. "The Backfire Effect: Why Facts Don't Win Arguments," bigthink.com. The original research was by Brendan Nyhan

of the University of Michigan and Jason Reifler of Georgia State University, "When Corrections Fail: The Persistence of Political Misperceptions," presented at the American Political Science Association in 2006.

8. G. E. Moore, "Wittgenstein's Lectures in 1930–1933," in *Philosophical Papers* (London: George Allen and Unwin, 1970), 314.
9. Alice Crary, *Beyond Moral Judgment* (Cambridge, MA: Harvard University Press, 2007), 45. Hereafter cited parenthetically as *BMJ*.
10. Harold von Hofe, *Der Anfang* (New York: Holt, Reinhardt, and Winston, 1963).
11. Martha Nussbaum, *Cultivating Humanity: A Classical Defense of Reform in Liberal Education* (Cambridge, MA: Harvard University Press, 1997).
12. Ibid., 85.
13. Ibid., 86.
14. John Gardner, *On Moral Fiction* (New York: Basic Books, 1978), 19.
15. Epictetus, *Enchiridion,* XLVI, trans. George Long (Amherst, NY: Prometheus Books, 1991), 40.
16. Plato, *Plato: Collected Dialogues,* trans. and ed. Edith Hamilton and Huntington Cairns (New York: Pantheon Books, 1961), 771.
17. Cf. Thomas Moran, *The Exchange of Words: Speech, Testimony, and Intersubjectivity* (Oxford: Oxford University Press, 2018).
18. Thomas Reid, *Essays on the Active Powers of Man,* essay 5, "Of Morals," chapter 6 "Of the Nature and Obligation of a Contract."

4. WHAT IS THE LIBERAL ARTS CANON AND HOW IS IT JUSTIFIED?

1. Moore, "Wittgenstein's Lectures in 1930–1933," 314.
2. Alasdair MacIntyre, *After Virtue: A Study in Moral Virtue* (South Bend, IN: University of Notre Dame Press, 1981), 207.
3. Professor Donald C. Reed, private communication.

4. Jaroslav Pelikan, "King Lear or Uncle Tom's Cabin?" in *The Teaching of Values in Higher Education* (Washington, DC: Woodrow Wilson Center, 1985).
5. Joseph Conrad, *Lord Jim* (New York: Barnes and Noble Classics, 2004), 170–71.
6. Wallace Stevens, "Of Mere Being," in *The Palm at the End of the Mind: Selected Poems and a Play* (New York: Alfred A. Knopf, 1971), 398.

5. LIBERAL ARTS IN A GLOBAL CONTEXT

1. Bertrand Russell, *Introduction to Mathematical Philosophy* (New York: Simon and Schuster), 169–70.
2. Karl Marx and Friedrich Engels, *Communist Manifesto* (New York: Charles H. Kerr, 1906).
3. Thomas Hardy, *The Woodlanders* (New York: Harper and Brothers, 1905), 52.
4. George Eliot, *Adam Bede* (New York: Everyman's Library, 1906), 569.

6. LIBERAL ARTS AND PERSONAL IDENTITY

1. Homer, *The Odyssey*, trans. W. H. D. Rouse (New York: Mentor Books, 1937), 66.
2. Thomas Fuller, in *The New Dictionary of Thoughts: A Cyclopedia of Quotations from the Best Authors of the World, Both Ancient and Modern*, ed. Tyron Edwards (London: Classic Books, 1937), 257.
3. William Wordsworth, *Works*, ed. Stephen Gill (Oxford: Oxford University Press, 1984), 611.
4. Ibid., 598.

5. Albert Camus, *The Myth of Sisyphus,* trans. Justin O'Brien (New York: Vintage, 1955), 91.
6. Brenda Magnus, *Nietzsche's Existential Imperative* (Bloomington: Indiana University Press, 1978), 154.
7. Friedrich Nietzsche, *Thus Spoke Zarathustra,* trans. Walter Kaufmann (New York: Penguin Books, 1954), 162.
8. Friedrich Nietzsche, *The Will to Power,* trans. Anthony M. Ludovici (Edinburgh: Foulis, 1910), 48.
9. Nietzsche, *Thus Spoke Zarathustra,* 219.
10. Alexander Nehamas, *Nietzsche: Life as Literature* (Cambridge, MA: Harvard University Press, 1986), 150. Hereafter cited parenthetically as *NLL.*
11. See Wendell Berry, *The Unsettling of America* (New York, Avon, 1977), 125.

BIBLIOGRAPHY

Aeschylus. *The Orestes Plays of Aeschylus: The Agamemnon; The Libation Bearers; The Eumenides.* Translated by Paul Roche. New York: Mentor Books, 1962.

Aristotle. *Nicomachean Ethics.* Indianapolis: Bobbs-Merrill, 1993.

Bacon, Francis. *Novum Organum.* In *The English Philosophers from Bacon to Mill,* edited by E. A. Burtt. New York: Modern Library, 1939.

Barnes, Julian. *The Sense of an Ending.* New York: Alfred A. Knopf, 2012.

Berry, Wendell. *The Unsettling of America.* New York: Avon, 1977.

Bevis, Matthew. "I Can Bite Anything I Want." *London Review of Books,* July 16, 2015.

Bombay, Scott. "Surveys: Many Americans Know Little about the Supreme Court." National Constitution Center. February 17, 2016. https://constitutioncenter.org/blog/surveys-many-americans-know-little-about-the-supreme-court/.

Boswell, James. *The Life of Samuel Johnson, L.L.D.* New York: Modern Library, n.d.

Burns, Robert. "To a Louse: On Seeing One on a Lady's Bonnet at Church." In *Complete Works,* 1786. robertburns.org.

Camus, Albert. *The Myth of Sisyphus.* Translated by Justin O'Brien. New York: Vintage, 1955.

Carroll, Lewis. "The Hunting of the Snark." In *The Lewis Carroll Book,* edited by Richard Herrick. New York: Tudor, 1944.

———. "What the Tortoise Said to Achilles." *Mind,* 1895.

Chapman, Graham, John Cleese, Terry Gilliam, Eric Idle, Terry Jones, and Michael Palin. *The Complete Monty Python's Flying Circus: All the Words.* New York: Pantheon Books, 1989.

Conrad, Joseph. *Lord Jim.* New York: Barnes and Noble, 2004.

Crary, Alice. *Beyond Moral Judgment.* Cambridge, MA: Harvard University Press, 2007.

Descartes, René. *Discourse on Method.* In *The European Philosophers from Descartes to Nietzsche,* edited by Monroe C. Beardsley. New York: Modern Library, 1960.

Dickens, Charles. *Bleak House.* New York: Everyman's Library, 1907.

———. *David Copperfield.* New York: Modern Library, 1992.

Edmonds, David, and John Eidinow. *Wittgenstein's Poker: The Story of a Ten-Minute Argument between Two Great Philosophers.* New York: Ecco, 1990.

Edwards, Tyron, ed. *The New Dictionary of Thoughts: A Cyclopedia of Quotations from the Best Authors of the World, Both Ancient and Modern.* London: Classic Books, 1937.

Eliot, George. *Adam Bede.* New York: Everyman's Library, 1906.

———. "Essay on Thomas Carlyle." *The Leader,* October 27, 1855. Reprinted in *Essays of George Eliot,* edited by Thomas Pinney. New York: Oxford University Press, 1963.

Epictetus. *Enchiridion.* Translated by George Long. Amherst, NY: Prometheus Books, 1991.

Fendrich, Laurie. "I Argue, Therefore, I Am." *Chronicle Of Higher Education,* July 21, 2011.

Fish, Stanley. *Save the World on Your Own Time.* Oxford: Oxford University Press, 2012.

Fogelin, Robert J. *Evidence and Meaning.* New York: Routledge, 1967.

Forster, E. M. *Howard's End.* New York: Vintage Books, 1989.

Gardner, John. *On Moral Fiction.* New York: Basic Books, 1978.

Gardner, Martin, ed. *More Annotated Alice: Alice's Adventures in Wonderland and through the Looking Glass.* 1990.

Gilliam, Terry, and Terry Jones, dirs. *Monty Python and the Holy Grail*. 1975.

Grahame, Kenneth. *The Wind in the Willows*. New York: Holt, Rinehart, and Winston, 1980.

Hardy, Thomas. *The Woodlanders*. New York: Harper and Brothers, 1905.

Hartley, L. P. *The Go-Between*. New York: New York Review Books, 1953.

Hayden, Michael. "The End of Intelligence." *New York Times*, April 29, 2018.

Heraclitus. *Fragments*. Translated by T. M. Robinson. Toronto: Toronto University Press, 1987.

Homer. *The Odyssey*. Translated by W. H. D. Rouse. New York: Mentor Books, 1937.

Hofstadter, Douglas. *Gödel, Escher, Bach*. New York: Basic Books, 1979.

Hume, David. *A Treatise of Human Nature*. Edited by L. A. Selby-Bilge. Oxford: Oxford University Press, 1951.

James, William. *The Varieties of Religious Experience*. New York: Modern Library, 1902.

Kierkegaard, Soren. *Soren Kierkegaard's Journals and Papers*. Edited and translated by Howard V. Hong and Edna H. Hong. Bloomington: Indiana University Press, 1967.

Kuhn, Thomas S. *The Structure of Scientific Revolutions*. Chicago: University of Chicago Press, 1962.

Landis, John, dir. *Animal House*. Featuring John Belushi et al. 1978.

Louie. "Baking Grandma's Bread." https://www.traditionaloven.com/46/how-grandma-baked-delicious-breads.

MacIntyre, Alasdair. *After Virtue: A Study in Moral Virtue*. South Bend, IN: University of Notre Dame Press, 1981.

Magnus, Brenda. *Nietzsche's Existential Imperative*. Bloomington: Indiana University Press, 1978.

Marx, Karl, and Friedrich Engels. *Communist Manifesto*. New York: Charles H. Kerr, 1906.

McEwan, Ian. *Atonement*. New York: Anchor Books, 2003.

McGuinness, Brian. *Wittgenstein: A Life.* Vol. 1, *Young Wittgenstein, 1889–1921.* Berkeley: University of California Press, 1988.

Millar, A. C. *Hendrix College Catalogue.* 1890.

Monk, Ray. *Wittgenstein: The Duty of Genius.* New York: Free Press, 1990.

Moore, G. E. "Wittgenstein's Lectures in 1930–1933." In *Philosophical Papers.* London: George Allen and Unwin, 1970.

Moran, Thomas. *The Exchange of Words: Speech, Testimony, and Intersubjectivity.* Oxford: Oxford University Press, 2018.

Nehamas, Alexander. *Nietzsche: Life as Literature.* Cambridge, MA: Harvard University Press, 1986.

Nietzsche, Friedrich. *Thus Spoke Zarathustra.* Translated by Walter Kaufmann. New York: Penguin Books, 1954.

———. *The Will to Power.* Translated by Anthony M. Ludovici. Edinburgh: Foulis, 1910.

Nozick, Robert. *Philosophical Explanations.* Cambridge, MA: Harvard University Press, 1981.

Nussbaum, Martha C. *Cultivating Humanity: A Classical Defense of Reform in Liberal Education.* Cambridge, MA: Harvard University Press, 1997.

Nyhan, Brendan, and Jason Reifler. "When Corrections Fail: The Persistence of Political Misperceptions." Presented at the American Political Science Association, 2006.

Overview: History of the Gifford Lectures. https://www.giffordlectures.org/overview.

Pascal, Blaise. Thoughts, #72, "Man's Disproportion." In *The European Philosophers from Descartes to Nietzsche,* edited by Monroe C. Beardsley. New York: Modern Library, 1960.

Pelikan, Jaroslav. "King Lear or Uncle Tom's Cabin?" In *The Teaching of Values in Higher Education.* Washington, DC: Woodrow Wilson Center, 1985.

Pirsig, Robert. *Zen and the Art of Motorcycle Maintenance.* New York: Morrow, 1974.

Plato. *Plato: Collected Dialogues.* Translated and edited by Edith Hamilton and Huntington Cairns. New York: Pantheon Books, 1961.

Reid, Thomas. *Essays on the Active Powers of Man.* Wolcott, NY: Scholar's Choice, 2015.

Roberts, David. "America Is Facing an Epistemic Crisis." *Vox,* November 2, 2017.

Russell, Bertrand. *Introduction to Mathematical Philosophy.* New York: Simon and Schuster, Touchstone Books.

——. "Some Philosophical Contacts." In *Portraits from Memory.* New York, Clarion Books, 1956.

Small, Helen. *The Value of the Humanities.* Oxford: Oxford University Press, 2013.

Smith, Adam. *The Theory of Moral Sentiments.* Edited by D. Raphael and A. MacFie. Oxford: Clarendon, 1976.

——. *The Wealth of Nations.* New York: Bantam Classics, 2003.

Sophocles. *Antigone.* In *The Three Theban Plays,* translated by Robert Fagles. New York: Penguin Books, 1984.

Stevens, Wallace. "Of Mere Being." In *The Palm at the End of the Mind: Selected Poems and a Play,* 398. New York: Alfred A. Knopf, 1971.

Streng, Frederick J. *Emptiness: A Study in Religious Meaning.* Nashville: Abingdon, 1967.

Taylor, Peter. *A Summons to Memphis.* New York: Alfred A. Knopf, 1986.

Von Hofe, Harold. *Der Anfang.* New York: Holt, Reinhardt, and Winston, 1963.

Whitman, Walt. "Song of Myself." In *Leaves of Grass.* New York: Modern Library, 1993.

Williams, William Carlos. "Asphodel, That Greeny Flower." In *Asphodel, That Greeny Flower and Other Love Poems.* New York: New Directions Paperbacks, 1994.

Wittgenstein, Ludwig. "A Lecture on Ethics." *Philosophical Review,* January 1965.

——. *On Certainty.* Edited by G. E. M. Anscombe and G. H. Von Wright. Translated by Denis Paul and G. E. M. Anscombe. Oxford: Basil Blackwell, 1969.

——. *Philosophical Investigations*. Translated and edited by G. E. M. Anscombe. New York: Macmillan, 1958.

——. *Tractatus Logico-Philosophicus*. Translated by D. F. Pears and B. F. McGuinness. New York: Humanities, 1961.

——. *Zettel*. Edited by G. E. M. Anscombe and G. H. Von Wright, translated by G. E. M. Anscombe. Oxford: Basil Blackwell, 1967.

Woolf, Leonard. *The Journey Not the Arrival Matters: An Autobiography of the Years 1939 to 1969*. London: Hogarth, 1969.

Wordsworth, William. *Works*, edited by Stephen Gill. Oxford: Oxford University Press, 1984.